INTERVIEW PREPARATION

Questions Answers Skills and Techniques to Effectively Get Hired for the Job You have Been Hunting

By Richard McKee

© **Copyright 2019 - All rights reserved.**

The contents of this book may not be reproduced, duplicated or transmitted without direct written permission from the author.

Under no circumstances will any legal responsibility or blame be held against the publisher for any reparation, damages, or monetary loss due to the information herein, either directly or indirectly.

Legal Notice:

This book is copyright protected. This is only for personal use. You cannot amend, distribute, sell, use, quote or paraphrase any part of the content within this book without the consent of the author.

Disclaimer Notice:

Please note that the information contained within this document is for educational and entertainment purposes only. Every attempt has been made to provide accurate, up to date and reliable information. No warranties of any kind are expressed or implied. Readers acknowledge that the author is not engaging in the rendering of legal, financial, medical or professional advice. The content of this book has been derived from various sources. Please consult a licensed professional before attempting any techniques outlined in this book.

By reading this document, the reader agrees that under no circumstances is the author responsible for any losses, direct or indirect, which are incurred as a result of the use of information contained within this document, including, but not limited to, —errors, omissions, or inaccuracies.

INTRODUCTION   7
CHAPTER ONE 9
How to Get an Interview. Resumes and Covering Letters Social Media and More   9
Resumes   9
Cover Letters   10
Social Media and Online Profiles   12
CHAPTER TWO   18
Personal Preparation   18
Preparing for the Big Interview   21
CHAPTER THREE   26
Tell Me More About Yourself   26
Why Are You Interested in this Job?   26
Reason for the Question 26
How to Answer 26
Answer Examples   28
Similar Questions you Could be Asked   30
Things you Should Never Say   31
Why Are You Interested in this Job?   31
Reason for the Question 31
Answer Examples   32
Things you Should Never Say   35
In Summary   35
CHAPTER FOUR   36
Tell Me About Your Current or Most Recent Job Role   36
 Why Are You Looking for A New Job?   36
Reason for the Question 36
Answer Examples   37
Similar Questions You Could be Asked   40
Other things you should never say   41
In summary   42
CHAPTER FIVE   43
What Are Your Greatest Strengths?   43
What Are Your Biggest Weaknesses?   43
How to Answer the Question   43
Answer Examples   47
Things you Should Never Say   50
Similar Questions You Could be Asked   50
What are Your Biggest Weaknesses?   51
Reason for this Question   51
How to Answer 51
Answer Examples   52
Similar Questions You Could be Asked   55
Things You Should Never Say   55
In Summary   55
CHAPTER SIX 57
Why Do You Want to Work for Us?   57

What Do You See Yourself Doing in Five Years Time?   57
Reason for the Question 57
How to Respond   58
Answer Examples   59
Similar Questions You Could be Asked   61
Reason for the Question 61
How to Respond   61
Answer Examples   62
Similar Questions you Could be Asked   65
In Summary   65
CHAPTER SEVEN   66
How Do You Handle Stress and Pressure?   66
Why Should We Hire You?   66
Reason for the Question 66
How to Respond   67
Answer Examples   67
Similar Questions you Could be Asked   70
Reasons for the Question   71
How to Respond   71
Answer Examples   71
Similar Questions you Could be Asked   74
In Summary   74
CHAPTER EIGHT   75
What Are Your Hobbies and Interests?   75
What Are You Passionate About?   75
Reasons for the Question   75
How to Respond   76
Answer Examples   79
Reason for the Question 81
How to Respond   81
Answer Examples   82
Conclusion   84
CHAPTER NINE   85
Questions About Your Education   85
Questions About Your Experience   85
Reasons for the Question   85
How to Respond   86
Answer Samples   87
Questions you Could be Asked   89
Reasons for the Question   89
How to Respond   89
Answer Examples   91
Questions you Could be Asked   94
Conclusion   94
CHAPTER TEN 95
The Tough Interview Questions 95
Previous Bosses, Supervisors and Co-workers   95

Answer Examples 97
Questions you Could be Asked 100
People Skills and Working with Others 100
Answer Examples 101
Career Goals 103
How to Respond 103
Answer Examples 104
Other Questions You Could be Asked 106
In Summary 106
CHAPTER ELEVEN 107
Some Less Common Interview Questions 107
More unusual questions 110
In Summary 115
CHAPTER TWELVE 116
How to Handle Inappropriate or Illegal Interview Questions 116
In Summary 120
CHAPTER THIRTEEN 121
What Are Your Salary Expectations? 121
Have You Any Questions to Ask Me? 121
Reasons for the Question 121
How to Respond 122
Answer Examples 123
Similar Questions You Could be Asked 126
Reason for the Question 126
How to Respond 127
In Summary 131
CHAPTER FOURTEEN 132
More Than Just Answering Questions 132
In Summary 137
CONCLUSION 138
References 144

INTRODUCTION

Welcome to this book on "Interview Preparation" where we will be looking at questions, answers, skills, and techniques to effectively get hired for the job you have been hunting.

This book can help you if:

- You have a job interview coming up
- You're looking for a new job
- You have never had a job interview before
- You want to improve your interview technique

No matter whether you are about to attend your first job interview or your tenth, job interviews can always seem quite daunting. Many doubts can run through your mind. Will you be able to answer all the questions? Will you mess up? Will the sweat be dripping off your hot red face? Will you say something stupid? Will your nerves get the better of you? All these concerns are entirely valid, and I have interviewed candidates who I am sure must have left the interview kicking themselves for some of their responses or actions.

In this book, we will look at how to ensure none of these problems arise and you can be a competent, self-assured, dynamic and exciting candidate that can demonstrate to the employer why you are right for the job.

You will learn how to:

- Get the knowledge you need to answer questions fully
- Stay calm and focused
- Be positive and engaging
- Showcase the best points of your personality
- Write a resume and covering letter that will get you noticed
- Prepare yourself mentally and physically for the interview

- Answer the most commons questions
- Know why the interviewer is asking the questions
- Respond in the best ways to the questions
- Answer even the tough interview questions and know how to handle them
- Answer the less common interview questions and know how to prepare yourself
- Deal with illegal questions
- Negotiate your salary
- Prepare yourself in other ways before the interview

Many people enter job interview totally unprepared and therefore unable to answer the questions put to them in the best way. I will help you learn how you can ensure this doesn't happen to you and give you the tools necessary to formulate excellent responses to every question, no matter how difficult or bizarre the questions asked may be.

I hope you find this book beneficial in helping you land your ideal job and that your interviews are successful.

Before you start reading further, it would mean a lot to me, if you would take the time to leave a review on the book if you end up finding it useful. In this way, you will be helping more people in seeing it and getting the information they have been looking for.

Please now read on to find out more.

CHAPTER ONE

How to Get an Interview. Resumes and Covering Letters Social Media and More

This book isn't about how to write the most fantastic resume or covering letter, but it is wise to remember when you start looking for a new job, that you're effectively marketing yourself. Every aspect of your pre-interview information, including your resume, cover letter, social media profiles, application site information, and references need to be targeted towards the jobs you are applying for. By getting things right here, you'll have done most of the leg work before you even attend an interview.

A strong, visual, clearly laid out resume and well-structured covering letter will help to get you noticed over other applicants. They need to show that you're the right person for the job.

Resumes

On average your resume will probably only be scanned for between 15 to 30 seconds by any potential employer. In those precious few seconds, you will be judged, so it is essential that the key information is easy to see, brief and to the point and draws visual focus. It must communicate your skills and highlight the value you could bring to the company.

A resume should succinctly contain the following:

- Your experience. This includes past employment or non-paid experience, such as voluntary charity work
- Your education and qualifications
- Your accomplishments. Promotions, awards, and other recognition

- Your attributes, such as team player, communicator, team leader, research skills, problem-solving ability and so on

All these things should quickly emphasize, not only your relevant accomplishments, but also the potential contributions you could bring to the role you're applying for.

Focus only on things that are relevant to the job you're applying for and leave out the rest. You're aiming for clear, concise, organized, easy to read information that can tell your potential employer everything at a glance.

Other things that can help to make your resume stand out is using attention-grabbing bold headlines that are in a different color, font, and size to the body text. These could be experience, attributes, qualifications, interests and so on.

Adding a headshot photo is another excellent touch as following your interview when the company is selecting their final potential candidates it will help them to remember you.

The end result should be a resume that has an impact, is well laid out and gives you're an air of professionalism – so spell check it and ensure there are no silly mistakes more than once. Getting someone else to look is a great idea too. You'll be able to find example resumes and even resume templates online. Choose one that you think looks good and use it as an example to copy the layout structure.

Remember whenever possible your resume should only be one sheet of paper and no more, this is why putting only the most relevant information and not your entire life history on it is so important.

Cover Letters

It is a regular practice to also include a cover letter or letter of introduction with your resume. The covering letter allows you to elaborate on the information you gave in your resume and show some of your personality in the way you write.

Covering letters shouldn't be a stock letter you send out to all the jobs you are applying to. Instead, it would help if you took the time to personalize each one. This doesn't just mean changing the address on the letter but means directing it to the correct person within the company and structuring it in such a way that it applies to both the role you are applying for and the company itself, acknowledging their values.

Unfortunately, not all potential employers will read all the covering letters, which is why your resume must stand out from the crowd.

Covering letters should convey who you are, the position you're applying for, how employing you would benefit the company and why you are interested in the job. It should be well written, concise but thorough and shouldn't exceed one page in length.

Use the job description to help you with the tone of the letter and make sure you check out the business's website so you can reflect the vibe of the organization and include relevant details to your letter.

You can match the design style of your letter to your resume, but ensure you use a professional business layout for standard business letter writing, with correct salutations.

Your opening paragraph should specify who you are, the position you're applying for and something of interest about how you were attracted to the job/company and how you heard about the job.

The middle paragraphs you should highlight your experience, accomplishments, qualifications and why you believe you are the right fit for the job. Using examples to demonstrate this is a good idea. Use the company's mission statement to explain further why you're the one as your skillset closely matches the organization's needs.

In the final paragraph thank the reader for considering you for the position and reaffirm your interest in the company and position they are advertising.

Ensure that your name, telephone number, physical address and email address are clearly marked on the letter.

Lastly, CHECK YOUR SPELLING AND GRAMMAR! First impressions are so critically important, letting something as simple as poor spelling and grammar let you down is unnecessary.

Social Media and Online Profiles

It is wise to remember that looking you up on social media is easy to do. So, if you don't want your potential employer seeing all your party animal posts and photos ensure that you have the correct security measures set up on your profile.

It is, however, advantageous to have a great business-specific social media profile that is again linked in style to your resume but can also contain a more considerable amount of information about what you have done, your interests and previous accomplishments in all fields. You can use as many of the different platforms as you like including LinkedIn, Twitter, Facebook, Pinterest, YouTube, Instagram or Snapchat. Depending on the type of work you do, will generally steer you to the most appropriate social media platforms to highlight what you do.

There are more to consider than just social media profiles online. There are also job boards, groups and employment systems that you might use to search for that perfect job. Ensuring that all your profiles match to tell the same story is important, as an employer might find it confusing if you have seemingly different information in different places.

These are the things to keep in mind when you are creating your online profiles:

- Images. Use good quality headshots and photos that reflect who you are and what you can do.
- Names. Select a username that is professional, not cute or clever.
- Promotion. Talk about your skills, experience, and accomplishments and elaborate on the kind of jobs you would like to do.
- Targeting. If you're going to use job boards, ensure that you keep the information concise and targeting to the roles you are looking for to help potential employers find you more easily.
- Links. Link as many things as you can, websites, social media, portfolios and so on.
- Update. Ensure that you regularly update the information to keep your profile fresh and up to date.
- Privacy. As I mentioned earlier, protect your privacy and review the privacy settings regularly. Also, ensure you renew passwords frequently and don't make them all the same. I simply use an address book to keep track of all my passwords. It is safe and efficient. However, if you do want to keep them online, you can use a password app to keep them safe and accessible

LinkedIn

If you don't already have a LinkedIn profile, then it is easy to build one by visiting the site.

Include the site to your advantage by:

- Detailing all the information within your resume
- Use the most relevant keywords to highlight your skill and accomplishments
- Use a professional headshot image on your profile
- Find organizations to follow that interest you so you are updated about any opportunities

- Join any relevant groups that apply to your career field and stay up to date with the latest trends
- Search for any alumni that are in organizations you might like to work for. Connect with them and ask if they can provide you with information that might be beneficial
- Keep your profile up to date

Facebook

Facebook is great for keeping in touch with friends and family, but it is also a fantastic network marketing tool. It is advisable to create two profiles, one professional and one personal.

- When you build your Facebook page just as with LinkedIn, ensure you use a good quality headshot as this makes you appear professional
- Post some information on your page about your business self and career
- Join groups that are focused on your career interests and get involved in them by asking questions and commenting on other members questions
- Join any Facebook pages run by organizations you are interested in, as this can be a great insight to what that business is all about and provides you with information such as their latest job listings
- Ensure your privacy settings are set only to allow the people you want to view your information to see it

Twitter

Twitter is a useful tool to learn about organizations through their directors and managers. You can create your own "tweets" or respond to "tweets" from others. This can help you to create useful connections and build your professional image.

- Start by setting up an account and create your unique twitter handle. This could be part of your name mixed with your profession as an example. You can be as creative as you like but try to make it relevant in some way
- Add your headshot
- Build a great profile that highlights all your professional skills and accomplishments
- Add links to your websites, portfolios or work samples
- Create and respond to tweets that demonstrate your knowledge and the interests you have within your field
- Follow any businesses and organizations you are interested in and keep a lookout for any tweets that you can jump in on
- To strengthen connections re-tweet, use direct messages and respond to any you receive
- Look for hashtags that are of interest to you such as #job offers and hashtags that belong to organizations you are interested in

Pinterest

Pinterest may not be your first thought when it comes to jobs and careers information, but if you are in a creative industry such as graphic design, cabinet making, or even landscape gardening then Pinterest is a fantastic way to not only show off your talents but also connect with businesses that might be interested in them.

- Set up your profile again using a professional image
- If you have created a striking modern infographic style resume, then add it to your page
- Create boards featuring your work that highlight your strongest pieces arranged into categories that make it clear about the content
- Link your pages to portfolios, videos, or other projects

- Ensure you carefully label the images you upload so that it helps search results and people can find your work more easily
- Follow others who inspire you and people whom you would like to work for if they have accounts

Online Portfolios

If your work is visual, then create an online portfolio. Several sites are offering this service online, or you can simply create your own website.

You should show examples of your work that demonstrate your ability, knowledge, and skills. This can be very beneficial as it allows employers to really get a feel of what you can do.

Don't forget to add links to your portfolio on your other online and social media sites.

Writing Portfolio

Just as with a creative visual portfolio for artists, graphic designers, furniture makers and so on, you can also build a portfolio if you are a writer. This doesn't mean you have to add hundreds of full-length documents, but you can include "snippets" from interesting work you have written. Make sure that you inform how you write, so talk about how you research your work and keep content fresh and exciting.

Include the best work you have written:

- Press releases
- Website content (including links to the site where possible, but get permission from the owner of the site first)
- Examples of brochures or leaflets
- Copy you have written
- Articles
- Blogs

- Book extracts
- Any written work that showcases your writing talents

Once you have worked hard creating your "professional public image," then you will be ready to launch your search for the perfect job and will stand a far better chance of being selected for an interview.

CHAPTER TWO

Personal Preparation

When it comes to presenting yourself as the perfect candidate at a job interview, there is a lot more to it than just having a reasonable answer for all the questions you will be asked. How you answer the questions, your body language, eye contact, demeanor, and appearance will also add to the overall image you portray.

Many job applicant's work really hard on their resume and cover letter but are a total disappointment at the interview.

Not all of us feel confident and comfortable in an interview situation, and this can be made worse if your interview is in front of a panel rather than just with an individual. The only way to counter this so that you won't become tongue-tied, blush red as a beetroot or want to run from the interview room at the fastest available opportunity is to practice, practice, practice. Ask some friends to do mock interviews with you and give you their feedback on how you did. You can supply them with a list of questions to ask and ensure that they don't ask them in the order you gave them and tell them to throw in a few of their own too. By doing this even just a few times, you will quickly become more at ease about it and will hopefully be able to avoid feeling like a fool in a real interview.

Let's take a look at a couple of examples if you imagine you are the interviewer rather than the interviewee and there are just two applicants for the job. The first has an amazing CV and well written, informative cover letter. When they enter the room, you are at first struck by their disheveled appearance, and that stain on their shirt just keeps drawing your attention. You welcome them shaking their hand and ask them to take a seat. You notice that they don't smile and only respond in whispered murmurs. Smiling back at them you thank them for attending the interview and explain that you felt they had a good resume. There is still no real response from them as they gaze at the floor, seemingly afraid to make eye contact with you. You commence with your first question, "Tell me about yourself." They continue to look at the floor flashing occasional glances up to you and mutter something, which is practically inaudible. You apologize and ask if they would mind speaking up a little. This continues for the entirety of the interview, and you can sense that all they really want to do is get out of the room. When it comes to the end of the interview, and you ask them if they'd like to ask you any questions, they shake their heads and virtually make a run for the door.

The second interviewee then enters the room. This person didn't have as strong a CV as the first applicant, having a lot less experience and training. You notice immediately how well turned out they are, clean, tidy, groomed. They smile at you and shake your hand firmly. They hold your eye contact and concentrate on what you are asking them. Their answers to your questions are well thought out, eloquent and well delivered. They are relaxed and at ease. At the end of the interview when you ask if they have any questions for you, they ask not one but several that show they have thought about what you have told them during the interview.

Following these two interviews, which candidate would you choose? Hopefully, it would be the second one, as although on paper they are the weaker candidate, their potential to become a good employee who is eager to learn and easy to work with seems far greater. However, it could just be that the first employee is shy and would do the job just as well as the second. Yet, first impressions count! So, do all you can to ensure that the first impression you give is a good one.

Another big no-no is the overconfident applicant as that is just as bad. People who come into an interview with a know it all, I am always right, I am better than all the rest attitude is equally as off-putting to an interviewer. Striking a happy balance of confident but affable is where you want to aim for.

Personal Appearance

The visual image you give is vital in an interview. You will be judged on how you look.

Depending on the type of job you are applying for will change what is considered professional attire. If for instance, you are going for a position in an office environment, then wearing a business suit would be expected. If, however, you are going for a job as a welder, then clean overalls might be a better idea, particularly if you will be expected to demonstrate your skills. Whatever you decide is suitable attire, at the very least ensure it is clean, tidy and smells fresh. It isn't just visible dirt that is off-putting, bad odors are also unpleasant, so make sure it's washed.

It isn't just your attire, but yourself that matter too — clean, tidy hair, clean face, hands, fingernails and so on. If you are a woman, then keep makeup light and natural looking. You want to be remembered for your skills, eloquence, and manner, not for your dirty clothes or overdone slap.

Employers will think if you don't care about how you look and present yourself that there is little chance you will care much about your job.

Persona

Some people stand out in interviews more than others. You DO want to stand out in an interview situation, but for all the right reasons. Smiling in a natural friendly way not only makes you look better, but it also encourages your interviewer to like you at a subconscious level. It will also help you to relax.

Smiling encourages positive interactions, makes you appear friendly and approachable, qualities that are important if you will be working closely with colleagues.

Mental Preparation

As we touched on earlier, practicing "mock interviews" with family or friends can help you feel comfortable. You can do a similar thing by using a phone to video yourself practicing your answers to potential questions. Alternatively, look at interview practice videos on YouTube. You may feel silly doing these, to begin with, but that's a good thing as that feeling of being uncomfortable and self-conscious is what you are trying to overcome in a real interview situation - so stick with it. Before long you will be able to hone your answers and give the perfect response confidently and articulately every time.

Preparing for the Big Interview

We are going to look at some steps you should take to ensure that your interview is a success and even if you don't land the job, you know that you made the best effort possible to do so. Don't be disheartened by an unsuccessful outcome as it is all great practice, and it could just be that you were just not quite the right fit for the job on offer. If you approach each interview with the same preparation and attention to detail, you will soon land your dream job.

1. **Skills and Qualifications**

Ensure the skills and qualifications detailed on your resume are matched to the specified job requirements.

You can do this by:

- Outlining the skills, knowledge, qualifications and previous experience listed in the job description.
- Look at where the role fits into the company hierarchy. Entry level, middle management, supervisory and so on

and make sure the tone and style of your resume reflect this.

2. Research Everything About the Business

By finding out all you can about a future employer, it allows you to know things about the company that less prepared candidates will not. This shows the interviewer that you are genuinely interested in what they do and are willing to put in some effort.

To find out more about a business you can:

- Take a close look at the company website and learn as much as you can from it
- Ask anyone else you know who works there if they can tell you about the organization
- Look at the products or services they provide
- Learn who their clients are
- Understand who's who in the management structure
- Check out what other people are saying about them online or look at websites such as CareerSearch, The Riley Guide or the Vault.
- From what you find out use the information to help you create some questions about the company to ask during the interview. The interviewer may answer some, but chances are some will be left for you to use to find out more.

3. Wardrobe and Appearance

Plan what you are going to wear to the interview in advance.

Here are some things to think about:

- Keep it neutral, professional business attire for office type work, or clean work wear if you are going to be needing to demonstrate your skills on the day

- Make sure shoes are comfortable, clean and suitable
- Even if it says business casual is OK for the dress code, looking smart and professional will give a better impression
- If you wear the most expensive business suit in the world, all the interviewer will remember about you is the dollop of egg yolk on your lapel. Make sure that your clothes are clean, ironed and stain free
- Similarly, a beautiful outfit won't disguise messy hair or filthy fingernails
- Don't assume you won't get a job if you have tattoos or piercings, some employers are judgmental about these things, but if that is the case you don't want to work for them anyway.

4. Be Prepared

Ensure you bring everything you might need with you, get it ready the day before so you aren't having to search for it when you should be leaving for the interview.

Things you might want to bring along include:

- Your resume printed on high-quality paper
- A notebook or pad and a pen that works
- Your references and contact details for referees
- Identity documents or other documents you might be required to complete an application form such as your social security details
- Your portfolio that demonstrates your best work (if the job requires it)

5. Non-Verbal Communication

Remember that it isn't just what you say that matters, non-verbal communication will tell an interviewer a lot about you.

Even things you do while in the waiting room before the interview may get reported back, so be professional always.

Things to remember about non-verbal communication:

- Be confident. Even if you are nervous use breathing techniques such as the inhale slowly through your nose to the count of five, hold the breath for the count of five and exhale slowly through your mouth to the count of seven. You can do this to calm nerves while waiting; no one will know you are doing it.

- When you enter the room smile at the interviewer! Shake their hand firmly and listen to their instruction attentively

- When you sit down, don't slouch in the seat, be comfortable but upright

- Don't fidget. Nerves can make you do things subconsciously such grind your teeth, play with your hair, tap your foot, rub your hands together and so on. Make yourself body aware, so you don't do these things

- Give appropriate eye contact, when someone is asking a question or speaking to you, you should be looking at them. When you give your answer or are talking to them, then it is okay to look away as you naturally would in a conversation, but don't stare at the floor. If you don't like direct eye contact, look at a point just above their nose instead

- Keep any of your belongings in a bag next to you while in the interview, don't put anything on their desk uninvited. You can ask if they would like to see your portfolio or references and so on if they don't ask for them, but only hand them to them when asked to do so

- Remember that your face conveys your feelings. Be careful what your face tells the interviewer and try to keep your feelings positive and don't overreact

6. **Questions**

Be sure to prepare some suitable questions to ask the interviewer about the job or the company. You can write them down and cross them off if they answer any naturally during the interview. By doing this, it will show you have done some homework and are a serious candidate.

Questions you might ask include:

- If there are any training programs and details about them
- What the level of staff turnover is within the company
- What they think makes the company a great place to work
- How work performance is evaluated within the company
- What opportunities are there for promotion within the company
- Information on the working culture
- If there are any organized social events
- What challenges the company is facing
- From what the interviewer has seen of your application and today's interview, can they advise you in any way how you might improve?
- If there are any reasons they believe you are not suited to the position you are applying for

CHAPTER THREE

Tell Me More About Yourself

Why Are You Interested in this Job?

The questions "tell me more about yourself" and "why are you interested in this job?" are, in one form or another, almost definitely going to occur during your interview.

Reason for the Question

Tell me more about yourself is generally one of the first asked. It is used for several reasons, and it is a topic you should know a lot about and be able to talk about comfortably, so it is an ice breaker to help you relax. It is to see if you will be a good fit within the company and have interests that will complement the job. It is also to get an insight into your personality.

How to Answer

To answer this question, you want to give the interviewer see why you would be an excellent fit for the job, and not tell them your entire life history or all about how cute Tiddles your cat is, or your social circle dilemmas. They are not being interviewed by you to be your friend, and neither are they your shrink. Keep it friendly, but professional. It is okay to reference your pets or friends, but they mustn't become the focus of your answer. The interviewer is looking for a general overview about you, a snapshot insight as to who you are. They do not want to hear your autobiography.

Start by talking about your education, hobbies or interests. Try to let them know what motivates you and makes you excited. Showcasing your personality can be a good thing, as the employer will hopefully be looking for someone who can direct some passion into their work. Be concise, yet thorough, but don't give away too much personal information.

A simple technique you can adopt to help you construct your answers is to use a formula present, past and future. This allows you by telling the interviewer what you are doing now. This could be your current job, course you are doing, hobby or interest.

Follow this by telling them how you got there, which might include details of your education, an internship or working as a volunteer if you were talking about your current job. Finish by telling them about your goals and what you hope to be doing in the future. If you can align how the position you are applying for corresponds to these future goals, so much the better.

Practice your answer to this question, get the feedback of friends and family and be confident about what you are going to say before the interview. Remember that you don't want to bore your potential new boss to death, so keep it informative, short and sweet. Remember also to be humble. Having an over-inflated opinion of yourself is highly off-putting to most employers.

Try to avoid potentially contentious subjects such as your religious or political beliefs and talking about any responsibilities or interests you have that take up a lot of your time, as you might make them wonder if you will have the time to commit yourself entirely to your job. If you are training to be an Olympic athlete, that's great, but perhaps don't tell your future employer that at the interview. Just mentioning you are interested in athletics will do. Try putting yourself in your interviewer's place and think about what they are most likely to want to hear.

The temptation to list all the qualifications and experience you have and although this information is useful, it is also not giving the employer an insight into you as a person, other than that you are perhaps a little egotistical, a quality they are likely not looking for.

Tell them about a hobby that you really love such as painting, singing, golf, running and so on. Telling them that you enjoy physical pursuits will demonstrate that you are active and health conscious. While reading, playing an instrument or playing chess could show that you have more intellectual qualities. Art, singing, theatre showcase your artistic side. Being involved in charity or voluntary work can demonstrate that you care about others and are committed to their welfare showing that you are compassionate, yet dedicated.

Whatever you do talk about, it's a good idea to choose something that isn't already mentioned on your resume as you are trying to show why your character and personality are a good fit for the job you are applying for. Be careful however not to be too over enthusiastic. The focus should remain on the position you are applying for.

Once you have shared your interests, you can then highlight how some of the skills involved are advantageous to your career goals and professional skills. Share some of your personal qualities that emphasize these skills in the workplace environment.

Answer Examples
- During my leisure time, I enjoy walking with my dog. We often meet new people who are also out walking their dogs. This provides a great common ground for initiating a conversation. I feel the ability to communicate well in both your private and professional life is an invaluable skill, to ensure clarity and transparency.

- I am a very active person, and I enjoy a variety of sports. I go jogging before work each morning as I find it relaxes me and prepares me for the day ahead. On weekends I volunteer with a local community children's group that provides activities to disadvantaged kids. This brings me a great deal of pleasure and allows me to feel I am giving something positive to help others.

Fill in your own answers here:

_____

_____

_____

_____

_____

_____

_____

_____

_____

_____

_____

_____

_____

_____

Similar Questions you Could be Asked

There are a few other questions that are on a similar theme, looking for more personal information about you. They could include questions such as these:

What hobbies or interests do you have?

For this question, you would simply state the facts and tell them what hobbies you have. You could also include why you find them enjoyable and if possible, link reasons why they are complementary to the job you are being interviewed for.

Avoid giving your potential boss a full breakout of your daily schedule and do not give them cause to think that any of your hobbies may be more important to you than your job.

What do you enjoy doing when you are not working?

This is a similar question to the one above but is a little more open, so could include things like spending time with family and friends, walking your dog and so on.

Again, please don't get too caught up in detail, keep names and other personal information private, they don't need to know the name of your best friend, children, partner and so on.

Have you ever done any traveling?

In companies that have an international client base having experience of other cultures and languages can be advantageous. If you traveled through Asia during a gap year at college then you are showing independence, a sense of adventure and possibly a propensity to enjoy things that an employer might not be so keen on.

If you were an au pair or a chalet maid in the Alps for instance, then this shows you were prepared to work hard to also have fun, which is a good quality.

Be careful not to say things like "Oh yes, I just work so I can afford to go on luxury holidays as often as possible." This kind of response would make an employer believe you probably won't take your work seriously and your mind will be elsewhere. It also implies that you will be requesting a lot of vacation time.

Did you enjoy your schooling and Education?

Here the employer is trying to see if you were a serious and conscientious student. It is a poor question to ask as some people who did not do so well in school thrive in the workplace.

If you were a straight A student, then you can say that you very much enjoyed your education and you are anxious to continue learning throughout your career.

If you were someone who struggled at school, you could say that your education was just a small part of the process that got you to where you are today and that you believe life lessons are often learned from living and not in the classroom.

Things you Should Never Say
When answering any questions such as these, avoid talking about your personal life. You should never mention any details about your partner, children or your spouse for example.

Why Are You Interested in this Job?
This question, or one very like it, is standard at almost any job interview. You will no doubt have genuine reasons for why you have applied for the position. Although you may not find detailing them is beneficial to your cause.

Reason for the Question
It is asked to ascertain if you really know what the job is about and all that it entails. This is your opportunity to show

that your set of skills are well matched to the responsibility of the position you are being interviewed for.

As I explained in chapter one, your resume and cover letter should already match the skills and qualifications required by the job description. This is your chance to build on this by filling out some of the information you provided further.

If the job description was a little scant on detail, try looking for other postings for similar jobs on websites and job boards. You can then use this information to see what the most common requirements are. Alternatively, you can do a general online search for the job title and see what results come up.

Please write down the list of required experience and skills and think how your own previous experience and skillset fulfills them.

You shouldn't talk about how you will gain any benefit from the job, such as more pay, increased holiday and so on. Instead, the emphasis should be more about how it matches your skill set. You are basically advertising yourself to make it clear how hiring you will be beneficial to the company. You could also include how you like the company's products or feel aligned to its mission statement and so on.

Using some psychology here can be useful, by professing how much you like a company, or its products will probably only strengthen your case.

Answer Examples

- I have been using your company's products for a long time and must say how much I like them. When I saw an opportunity for working in your X department, I jumped at the chance to try out for the position. I have

X years in a similar role at X and have all the qualifications and experience listed on the job description. In addition to this, I have also attended courses on X, which could prove of use in the role. I feel that as a package my skillset is ideally suited to the position.

- I feel your company is at the cutting edge in this industry and the opportunity of working for you really excites me. Your requirement for someone with X experience and a background in X matches my own, and I can also bring X to the table, which could be beneficial to your future business growth.

- I feel very close to your company mission statement as it holds many values that I believe in. For this reason, I would really like the opportunity to be part of its growth and development. I have a master's degree from X in X which gives me the right skill set and the charity work I have been involved in for the past X years has given me the exposure that could make me a strong asset to your business.

Write your own answers here:

You can expand on these types of response adding your skills and experience. Remember that an employer may be interviewing many people for the same role, so you must shine and be remembered for your all good qualities.

They may have scanned your resume and a cover letter briefly prior to your interview but will take a closer look when you back up the details held within it. As an example, if you were being interviewed for a job as a bank clerk you might say "I have x years of customer service experience and a keep aptitude for math. I enjoy problem-solving and paying great attention to detail. I believe these skills will make me an excellent candidate for this role".

Things you Should Never Say

Be careful not to mention that you want this job because you disliked your old one or someone who worked there. Always keep things professional.

Never put yourself down in any way. If you were struggling at your previous job and working too many hours and ended up feeling overwhelmed, you don't need to say this as the interviewer might think you won't be up to doing the job you are being interviewed for either.

In Summary

Talk about the qualities you have that complement the job description, such as team working, experience, qualifications adaptability and so on.

Your interview doesn't have to be all serious and boring either, break the tension and inject your personality with a light touch. When telling them about yourself relaying a funny story, that has a good point to it, is a great idea. However, keep in mind that you are not meant to be delivering a standup comedy routine either. Smiling, genuinely smiling, will do a great deal to convey your friendly, warm and outgoing nature.

CHAPTER FOUR

Tell Me About Your Current or Most Recent Job Role

Why Are You Looking for A New Job?

These two questions are also interview favorites that can get you into hot water if you don't prepare them carefully in advance.

If you enjoyed your last job and had a great boss and co-workers, then the chances are you'll have no difficulty at all in answering "Tell me about your current or most recent job role." The trouble starts if things were not quite so rosy and there were elements about it that you didn't enjoy. It is essential not to say anything too negative, but at the same time, you do want to be truthful, so thinking about how to correctly phrase your responses is important. The last thing you want your potential new boss to feel is that you are going to complain about the smallest thing and make yourself challenging to work with.

Reason for the Question

Tell me about your current or most recent job role. In truth it isn't your likes and dislikes they want to know about, it is a test of your character. By asking you this question they want to see what kind of personality you have, are you upbeat, enthusiastic, committed, a team player?

When answering why are you interested in this job the interviewer is looking to see if you have any real interest in the role or the company and if you have correctly matched your qualifications and experience to it.

It is possible to make even poor experiences seem like good ones; you can focus on all that is good and positive and keep attention neutral and a little less focused on any negative experiences.

Let's look at some examples to illustrate this.

Answer Examples

- **What you really feel** – You were a member of a team working for a company that was struggling, often as a team, you became very unmotivated due to the lack of support given to you, but you all pulled together as hard as you could to make things work.
  What you could say - I worked with a great team that knew how to pull together during times of crisis.
- **What you really feel** – Your team leader and your Manager were great, but the head of HR was horrid, and you always felt she had it in for you.
  What you could say - Most of the leadership team were excellent and built a wonderful rapport with all the employees, knowing everyone by name.
- **What you really feel** – You have been working in the same job for three years, your qualifications you have and the dedication and effort you have put into the job mean that you should be promoted to a higher position. When the perfect spot for you opened up, they hired someone from outside the company, which upset you and made you feel unappreciated. At the moment no further vacancies are likely to become available within the company.
  What you could say - I have decided to look for another position as I feel I am ready to face greater challenges and take on more responsibility. There are no vacancies available in my current workplace that would allow me to do this.
- **What you really feel** – You joined the company when you graduated college and despite having proven your

worth many times over, still, feel you are treated like a junior. Despite asking for more responsibility your boss just keeps telling you, in a parental tone, when you are ready, I will consider it. After two years of this, you have had enough and have decided that despite working for the company you need to find another job.

What you could say - I have worked at X since I graduated. I decided that if I am to expand my working experience that it is time to find a role within a new organization, so I can continue to learn and grow.

- **What you really feel** – You are working for an acquaintance that was kind enough to give you a job when you needed it. You are the only employee.

  What you could say - The business I am working for is very small and cannot offer me any advancement. I have enjoyed working there, but feel I need to find a larger company with greater opportunities for employee growth.

- **What you really feel** – The group of people you work with are great, and you all get on well. The problem is you hate the work you are doing and find is super dull. You've decided you need to find a different kind of work that is more enjoyable.

  What you could say - The team at X are amazing, but my career focus has changed, so I am looking for a position where I can pursue this further.

- **What you really feel** – You are working in a huge factory with hundreds of other employees. The work is monotonous, and you just feel like a tiny cog in a big engine. You want to feel more valued and that what you do is of importance to the company you work for.

  What you could say - The company I am currently working for is very large, and I feel anonymous. I think I am better suited to working in a smaller organization where I can be a more integral and valued member of the team.

- **What you really feel** – You have a master's degree in X and did an internship that helped you develop practical skills in the same field. When you moved away from the area you were unable to find a job in a similar field, so just took what was available. You miss what you trained to do and want to return to it. You have found an opening at a promising company.

  What you could say – My master's degree, skills, and training are not fully utilized in my current role. I am hopeful that working for you will allow me to make better use of them.

Write your own answers here:

_____

_____

_____

_____

_____

_____

_____

_____

_____

_____

If you are asked outright "what didn't you like about your last job" then you should be truthful, but also complimentary. Try using a compliment sandwich like this:

I enjoyed working as a member of a great team at X, although I felt some of my skills were at times overlooked. I learned a great deal while working there but feel it is now time to move on to greater challenges.

Similar Questions You Could be Asked
- How would working for us be better than your last job?
- What was the most rewarding/least rewarding thing about your last job?
- Why do you want to work for us?

As before, be truthful but complimentary, again try the compliment sandwich approach.

To give a fuller answer, try adding some of the skills and requirements detailed in the job description to your answers. As an example:

- I enjoyed the interaction with customers on the phone at my last job, but I would like to do more face to face work with the clients as I believe I would find it more enjoyable.

- I am fully trained to work with X software, but my current job has no requirement for this. I enjoyed working with this software in the past, and as it is something your company uses, I am looking forward to being able to utilize my skills.

Be aware not to "red flag" things to your potential new employer. For instance, if your previous job required you to cold call people to convert into customers and the job you are applying for does have an element of speaking to customers on the telephone, but to a far lesser extent than at your previous job. Do NOT mention that you hated having to do the cold calling, and please don't say you enjoyed it either, simply stay neutral about it saying that it formed part of the job. You could, however, use it to highlight that the job you are interviewing for would be preferable to your last one. For example, you might say "I enjoy working with customers, but I am pleased the job role at your company does not require any cold calling."

Other things you should never say

- Don't disclose that you did not get on with a co-worker or anyone connected to the company you have been working for, even if they are the reason you have decided to leave

- Don't disclose that you hated the job you do/did

- Don't ever make discriminatory remarks about the company you worked for or anyone within the company, even if it is common knowledge that they are not good. If the interview said to you "oh you poor thing, you worked for Mr. X, he has the worst reputation" all you would do is say that yes you did work for him but nothing further

- Don't say that your job was tedious, difficult, stressful, or use any other negative words to describe it

In summary

Stay positive. Even if you hated your previous job, you don't want to let any new potential employer know that.

By being upbeat, complimentary, and using positive language, you are far more likely to get hired than if you use negative language and tell the interviewer how miserable you were in your last job role.

Turn negatives into positives, or just don't discuss them at all.

CHAPTER FIVE

What Are Your Greatest Strengths?

What Are Your Biggest Weaknesses?

These two opposing questions are favorites in job interviews and need carefully considered responses.

Reasons for the Question

Your greatest strengths are generally fairly obvious to you. The interviewer wants to know what qualities and attributes you have that will make you a good fit for the job.

It can be difficult to answer this question, as often we are self-conscious when it comes to promoting ourselves. Being either overly modest or over inflated can both be detrimental.

The interviewer wants to know if your strengths are in line with the requirements of the job. Based on your response they will judge if you are the best applicant for the role. It is, therefore, necessary to consider your response as there would be no point highlighting your excellent event management skills if you are in fact being interviewed for a job as an accounts clerk.

How to Answer the Question

Discuss the attributes you possess that best match the characteristics you believe the employer is looking for from their job description, and other similar job descriptions in the same field. It is essential to show that you have the qualities they are looking for as if you don't meet with their criteria, they won't consider you for the position.

The best way to respond to the question is to describe each of your skills and highlight experience you have that demonstrates them.

The kind of general skills employers are looking for are broken out below.

Analytical skills

These types of skill demonstrate your ability to analyze information, solve problems and make decisions. These skills are required in almost every job situation and include:

- Problem-solving
- Logical thinking
- Creative thinking
- Adaptability
- Assessing the needs of customers or colleagues
- Being innovative
- Having good judgment
- Being open minded
- Having the ability to review and react to statistical analysis

Communication Skills

The ability to communicate effectively and appropriately with your colleagues, bosses, and clientele is an essential skill to succeed in business. Poor communication that promotes a lack of understanding, confusion, and misconception can lead to big problems. Excellent communication skills are one of the most critical for an organization to function to its fullest capability; they are often a skill that is not promoted highly enough.

By demonstrating that you have excellent communication skills, your future employer is assured that you will integrate well into the team and keep others apprised of all necessary information.

Communications skills can include:

- The ability to listen to others and act on their intel

- Keeping your team informed when changes occur, keeping everyone up to speed
- Being able to calm and empathize with agitated clients resolving their issues quickly and efficiently
- Being persuasive
- Speaking well in public
- Creating attention-grabbing copy for websites, articles, brochures and other business literature
- Designing a compelling presentation
- Excellent technical writing that can be understood easily by others

Dependability

Are you dependable? Can others rely on you? Employers are looking for employees they know they can depend on to be professional and responsible. That turn up for work on time and always complete work to a high standard by the designated deadline.

Dependability can be demonstrated by:

- Excellent time management
- Meeting deadlines
- Great attention to detail
- A determination to solve problems
- Achieving results above given targets
- Being highly motivated
- Finding alternative strategies when necessary
- Multitasking effectively
- Being respectful to everyone
- Having a strong work ethic
- Being success and results driven
- Having good tact and diplomacy
- Being respected by others and respecting others

Team working and Leadership Skills

Most jobs require you to work in a team. Because of this it is necessary that you are a team player and work in unison with the other members and not against them. If you are going into a management role, you will need to demonstrate your ability to lead a team effectively and manage problems as they arise.

Team working and leadership skills include:

- Managing all team members effectively
- Making decisions
- Communicating effectively with other team members
- Motivating your team
- Working efficiently towards common goals
- Mentoring
- Giving constructive criticism
- Conflict resolution
- Keeping teams on target

Information Technology (IT)

In today's world it is complicated to get away from the need for some level of IT skill requirement. Almost every job will demand that you can operate a computer at some level.

When talking about your IT skills try to give examples of practical applications you are used to performing and any qualifications you hold.

If the job description highlights the need for using a particular piece of software that you have not used, but you have used something very similar. It is worth saying that you are very familiar with the related piece of software and that as you are a quick learner, you will be able to adapt to their preferred software without a problem. Obviously, if you have never used the specified programs or anything remotely similar, then you will not have the necessary qualifications for the job.

Examples of IT skills include:

- Word-processing
- Email
- Social Media
- Databases
- Graphics such as Photoshop, Illustrator or InDesign
- Presentation tools such as PowerPoint
- Data management such as Access
- Spreadsheets such as Excel
- Accounting software such as Sage or QuickBooks
- Plus, other more specialist software

Narrow down your list of skills so that you have just three to five of your very strongest. This will make answering any additional information you are asked about them easier to answer. Try to include skills from the different categories so that your response is balanced and not overly heavy in one area.

Answer Examples

- I believe that dependability is one of my strengths. As an example, when I have deadlines to work to, I always plan to complete the project in advance. Doing this has two advantages, firstly it means most of my work is completed ahead of schedule which pleases the customers and secondly if a problem is encountered it allows times for the issue to be resolved and still bring the project in on time.

- My writing skills are one of my greatest strengths. I have been working as a business blogger for the past four years. I have been very fortunate, and my work has been featured on some of the top business writing sites such as Forbes and Mashable.

- I think dedication and hard work are two of my greatest strengths. I have over 11 years of experience within the sales market and have managed to exceed the company's sales goals each quarter significantly.

- Having worked in customer service for the past six years my ability to solve client's problems and provide a happy outcome even in the most trying of circumstances is a definite strength. I put this down to my ability to listen to the customers' needs and communicate effectively with them. I ensure their problems are resolved quickly and efficiently and keep them updated on progress. Providing this dedicated, caring customer service has helped the company I work for, to gain a reputation of trust within the industry. I am now responsible for training other customer service representatives to use the same methods, so the level of success is uniform.

- Although I am currently the marketing director at X, I started my career with the company as a packer in the warehouse. I was lucky that the company recognized my abilities and I have worked my way up through the company to where I am today. Along the way I have been able to build upon my strengths, proving that I was a motivated, diligent, responsible member of their team. I have attended courses to gained qualifications from attending night school and believe I have played a significant part in propelling the company from its humble beginnings, along with my own, to be one of the most successful in the country.

Write your own answers here:

Things you Should Never Say
Being humble is all very well on a first date, but a job interview isn't the place for it. It is true that you don't want to make yourself out to be an egocentric either so try to be confident and truthful about your best achievements.

Don't just utter a vague list of strengths giving no detail, such as "I'm reliable, dependable, honest, hardworking, conscientious, and a good learner." This tells your interviewer nothing of your worth and why you think you have these strengths. Formulate full answers such as the ones shown above.

Don't focus on the strength you may have that will have no bearing on the job you are being interviewed for. It is merely a waste of time.

Here are some examples of terrible answers:

- Everyone thinks I am incredibly intelligent. I am probably the best applicant you are interviewing. I'm also hardworking, and I'm just amazing at communicating.
- My greatest strengths are project management, budget development, event planning, and social media.

Similar Questions You Could be Asked
These could be questions such as:

- How do you think your strengths have helped you perform your job?
- Which of your strength will help you most with this job?
- How will you use your strengths in the first few months of starting this job?
- Which of your strength do you think make you the most successful at your job?

All of these can be answered if you have done your homework well enough on identifying your strengths and thinking about how you use them and examples of how they are a proven asset to you.

What are Your Biggest Weaknesses?
This is definitely an alarm bell ringing question, slipping up here could cost you dearly so ensure you have put thought into how to respond.

Reason for this Question
The interviewer is only partially interested in ascertaining your faults, they also want to see your ability to problem solve, and this question is, after all, a problem. The last thing you want to do is tell a potential employer what your faults are!

This is where having the ability to turn a fault into an asset comes into play as I will reveal.

How to Answer
One way of answering this troublesome question is to play a little politics. By this I mean do not confess to any shortcomings, instead talk about a weakness you had historically but then overcame.

An example of this could be, "As the HR Manager I had no interaction with our company's clients. I felt that to better understand the difficulties faced by our customer services representatives and our sales team that I should learn more about their roles. I took several online courses on customer services and sales skills and have learned a great deal. I am now involved in sales meetings and help set up training for our customer services team, if I hadn't done the training, I would not be able to do this effectively. I believe it has helped me be a better manager for my staff".

Another solution is to turn a negative into a positive. This can be done by using something that employers will see as an asset as your weakness. For example, "I am dedicated to ensuring that projects stay on schedule so they can be completed on time. I would say that perhaps I don't need to triple check all the details, but it is critical to me that the job is done right."

What is important here is that you are identifying that you believe this trait to be a fault and can manage it, so it doesn't interfere with productivity.

Never actually use the work weakness or any other negative words, always look for positive ways to answer.

Answer Examples

Here are a few examples you can adapt to suit your situation.

- In the past, I tended to try and do everything myself. I have learned that by delegating work, I can get a lot more done. I use a project management app that allows me to maintain a close watch on the progress of all the work I have delegated, and I am getting a lot more comfortable about letting go of the reins a bit more.

- I like to complete projects well ahead of their deadlines. This is great as I have never missed a deadline, but it can cause me to sometimes rush. I felt that this could sometimes mean the work wasn't up to a standard that I desired. I have now learned that by taking a little more time that I can still get the work in by the deadline and it is of a higher quality.

- I am not a naturally organized person. I tend to prioritize my tasks, favoring those that impact the bottom line rather than doing things I feel are of small importance such as clearing my desk or emptying my inbox. I have now learned that by taking a few minutes to see to those small tasks and to keep things organized better, it increases my productivity. To help me stay on top of this, I am now using a time management system, which allows me to stay organized without compromising my responsibilities.

- I used to leave setting appointment until the last possible minute, but I learned from a colleague that by scheduling them well in advance makes things a lot easier. This way I can organize my workflow around them better, and they interfere less with my productivity.

- I am not a particularly numerate person, but luckily this has no impact on my writing skills, which are the primary skill necessary for my job as a copywriter. I have over time started to become involved with the internet marketing side of things, and analytics is a big part of this. My fear of numbers has now turned into something of a fascination as I can see how useful the numbers can really be.

Write your own answers here:

Similar Questions You Could be Asked

- What part of the job would you find most challenging?
- Can you tell me how you have overcome your weaknesses?
- Tell me how you would have done something differently at work.
- What is the most common criticism about you?
- What upsets you most in the workplace?
- What is the biggest criticism you have received?

By understanding your true weaknesses, you can resolve them. You should work on your weaknesses or at least implement strategies that can help you overcome them. By saying this, you will show you are intelligent and just like every other human on the planet, not perfect.

Things You Should Never Say

Staying away from all negativity is important. Don't use the word weakness in your answer or any other words with the same meaning. Use positive language and describe how you have overcome any difficulties you have encountered in the past.

Don't try and be clever and say things like:

- My only fault is my modesty
- I am generous to a fault
- I am perfect in every way

And so on. Believe me, they will have heard it before, and it won't get you any points for originality or intelligence.

In Summary

These two questions are two of the most feared. However, by preparing yourself for them in advance and being confident of your answers, there is no need to worry.

Remember to use positive language, be confident and smile.

CHAPTER SIX

Why Do You Want to Work for Us?

What Do You See Yourself Doing in Five Years Time?

These questions are ever popular at interviews for any type of job. The reason you want to work for a company might be very straight forward and is simply that they pay more than your old employer. This probably isn't something you would want to confess to in such an obvious way, however. You also don't want to seem vague and give responses about how wonderful the company is, such as "I think the company is great" it must be backed up by reasons you think this.

The good old favorite of what do you see yourself doing in five years or some other time frame is generally rolled out in one form or another. Be careful here not to make the job you are being interviewed for is just a stop gap for another career you have planned in the future. Employers want dedicated employees that are invested in the company's future.

Reason for the Question

Why do you want to work for us? The employer is trying to determine which of the candidates really wants the job and how much you have found out about the company prior to the interview. They are looking for those who give a genuine response about being interested in the company and what it does. If you just want any old job so long as it pays the bills, fair enough, but that isn't what you want to say at an interview.

Employers want to believe that you will be enthusiastic about your work and will bring value to the company, not just be another mediocre employee who doesn't really want to be there and doesn't care about the company's aims or principals.

How to Respond

Ensure that you research the company thoroughly before your interview. It is okay to take notes into an interview with you if you think you might forget important information. Look at their website and read the company mission statement, who their clients are and the company structure. Find out about any products it sells and see how they are doing in the marketplace. You can also look for the company on LinkedIn, Facebook and other social media platforms as this will help you build up a better picture of what the businesses clients think about them and their products or services.

Once you have collated all the information think about how you could help the business. Consider any special skills you have that would be advantageous and remember not to stray too far from their mission statement. It is essential that you match your goals to those that are also the company's objectives.

To do this write a list of the company's primary objectives and then do the same aligning your own goals to them. If for example the company has a strong customer service ethic and wants to ensure their customers are always happy, ensure you note that as one of your own goals too.

Try not to get too ambitious and try to tick every box on their mission statement. It is better to choose just two things that can easily fit with the job you are going for and do an excellent job of explaining how you can help the company in those areas.

A common mistake when answering this question is to have a focus on what the company can do for you when what you should really be doing is focusing on what you can do for the company.

Answer Examples

Here are some example answers you can use to inspire answers of your own.

- I'm excited about working for you as your company is an industry leader. You've grown from strength to strength, and the responses customers are giving to your products on your social media sites show how enthusiastic they are about what you do. I already have a lot of experience from my previous job in a similar field, and I would love the opportunity to share my knowledge with you and be a part of seeing your company grow even more successful.

- A friend and former colleague of mine came to work for you last year. He's told me so much about the positive and co-operative ways your company works with its employees to improve their products and services. I think this is really refreshing and I would love the opportunity to bring my own expertise into the mixing pot. I feel with your way of working that many boundaries have been removed, that can, in a more traditional environment, prevent the creative process. My extensive experience and knowledge in computer-aided design will, I am sure, be advantageous to your business.

- Your mission statement really aligns to my own beliefs. I too want to make the world a better place for future generations and my experience in this field will complement your ethos perfectly.

- I have seen how your company has grown and is now expanding into the international market. I find this very exciting, and as my background is in global sales, I feel I would be a great asset in helping you achieve this aim.

Write your own answers here:
_____

_____

_____

_____

_____

_____

_____

_____

_____

_____

_____

_____

_____

Similar Questions You Could be Asked
There are a few similar questions or different ways of answering this question which include:

- "Why should we hire you?"
- "Sell yourself to me so that I want to hire you."
- "How will working for us help you?"
- "How will hiring you help us?"

For all these questions the same ideas apply, you want to show your knowledge of the company and its aims and elaborate on how hiring you will be beneficial.

Reason for the Question
What do you see yourself doing in five years' time?
This question is asked to see if you are interested in advancing your career and if you view that career advancement and being done with the company, or if you merely want to use the job as a stepping stone to further progress elsewhere. The interviewer wants to know if your career path is aligned to their company's goals and if you intend to make your career with them.

How to Respond
This is a difficult question to answer as after all how can any of us know what will happen in five years? The interviewer is aware of this, and so in truth, the question is purely hypothetical. They want to know right now what your intentions are but realize that over time this could change.

If you are looking to advance your career, then be honest and say that by working with them that you look forward to growing your career within the company. This does two things; it says that you are motivated and that you see yourself with them for the long term.

What you want to avoid is to let them know that you are only taking the job as a stop gap, or that you intend to use them to learn the industry so you can strike out on your own as a competitor. You need to show commitment and an interest in what they do, with a desire to make this achievable because they hire you.

Also, don't mention things like hobbies that are your possible future career choice or how you hope to make lots of contacts working for them.

However, you answer, ensure that you are not vague and that your goals align with the company's own, just as in the question "why do you want to work for us?". Research what a career path could look like from the entry point you would be starting with the company. Try to find out what is the average length a person would stay in that type of job. You can find this out by asking in forums on the Internet (but don't give out too many specifics about the job you are going for). You can look for information on job boards and within the company's website. You may also have friends or family who work in a similar role who could give you more information.

When answering start by telling the interviewer how you want to master the role for which they are interviewing you and then work your way up from there. Ensure that you include reasons why your skills, background, and interests will help you along the way.

It could be that the company you want to work for is to small for you to have any real opportunity for advancement. In this instant, you would instead say that you are looking forward to being a part of the company's growth and success over time and that in five years you hope you will have been instrumental in this.

Answer Examples

Here are a few examples of answers you can adapt to suit your circumstances.

- I would hope to have proven my worth with the company and been an integral part of its success. As I am highly dedicated to my work, I would like to have advanced within the company and hoped that I could over time continue to do so.

- As the company's international client list grows, I would like to think my background in global sales would have further advanced the company's growth in this area. I strive to know everything I can about the products I sell and form close relationships with clients. Because of this, I have managed to expand the client base quite rapidly, and many clients come on board from word of mouth. In recognition of providing the company with these things, I would hope that I might be able to run my own sales team.

When there are no opportunities for advancement you can use answers like these:

- I would like to think I will have been instrumental in growing the reputation of the company and significantly increasing its profits. My skills and experience can most definitely make this possible.

- I look forward to seeing how my involvement with the company has improved its output and increased the lines available. My specialist skills as an X will allow for dramatic expansion in this area, and this will I hope to add to the profitability of the company.

Write your own answers here:

You can add a lot more detailed information to your own answers to ensure that they are showing the best use of your talents and how this will help the business. Make sure you give examples of how you will achieve this.

Similar Questions you Could be Asked

Here are a few examples of similar questions you could be asked. To answer them use the same ideas as for answering, "what do you see yourself doing in 5 years?" Align your goals with the path of the company, detail your skillset that can make this achievable and give examples of how it could be done.

- What career goals do you have over the next five years?
- How are you planning to achieve your career goals?
- What are your long-term career goals?

In Summary

The trick with both questions is to find out as much as you can about the company in advance. Ensure that what you say aligns well with what the company is trying to achieve and highlight how you are going to make the company's goals achievable.

Avoid telling the interviewer that you see the job as a stepping stone to starting your own business. Alternatively, it is just a stopgap as what you intend to do long-term is something else entirely.

CHAPTER SEVEN

How Do You Handle Stress and Pressure?

Why Should We Hire You?

All jobs come with some level of stress and pressure, although the degrees of this can be very different depending on the career you choose. An attorney, for instance, is likely to feel a higher level of stress than an artist, but stress is undeniably present in all jobs.

The question why should we hire you? Can be difficult to answer as it is often embarrassing to sing your own praises. This is only a part of what the interviewer is looking for in response here, however, as they are also looking to see in what ways you believe you can help the company.

Reason for the Question
How do you handle stress and pressure? Here the interviewer wants to see your reaction if the job you are applying for is known to be a high-stress one and you have come from that background it is reasonable for them to assume that you have ways of dealing with it. If you are coming straight from college then you won't be experienced in the kinds of stress associated with the job, but you will have felt pressure and anxiety caused by exams, and this is where you can draw your answers from.

Stress is one of the biggest causes for employees to be off sick or quit their jobs. Showing that you are well able to deal with stress and have strategies you can employ to do so, will reassure your potential new boss that you are a safe bet.

How to Respond

Merely saying that you don't get stressed isn't going to cut it. We all get stressed, so saying you don't just isn't honest. What you need to do is provide examples of how you have coped with stress in the past. It can also be useful to give examples of how being under pressure makes you more productive.

Don't talk about situations where the stress you find yourself under is of your own making. Instead, talk about times when you have had to tackle complex assignments or been given very short deadlines, and you managed to find successful strategies to achieve your end goals.

Try not to talk about how being stressed affects you. Instead, turn the focus on how you overcame it. Also, be careful not to mention getting very stressed by work that will form a regular part of your new position should you be lucky enough to get the job.

By talking about how you manage to handle multiple projects all at once, despite having to juggle your workload to fit everything in, shows that you are forward thinking, good at problem-solving and can work on your feet changing your plans when needed.

You can also talk about how having a little bit of stress can help increase your creative thinking and team working efforts.

Answer Examples

Here are a few answers you can use to formulate ones to suit your own situation.

- I find that working under pressure makes me better at my job. My job as an analyst within a specialist department of the police force was highly pressured as accurate results were required fast. I found the pressure of this really helped me become highly focused on the task producing the results needed for the team.

- I enjoy a challenging working environment. I am used to meeting time critical deadlines while working on multiple projects. The pressure of the deadlines makes me really focus on the job and produces some of my most creative work.

- Having many assignments to complete or having deadlines that need meeting quickly motivates me and makes me more productive. I think this is good pressure. Sometimes when things don't go quite right, it can become a bit stressful, but that is when the team really come into their own as we all pull together to ensure the job not only gets done but gets done well. Over the years I've become adept at balancing multiple tasks at once, I think it is an essential skill. I can do this because I work out rigorous schedules that break down all the necessary work into easily manageable slices. By doing this, even the most overwhelming tasks become less daunting.

- Some projects can create stress within the team. I am susceptible to this and find that it can rub off on me. That is why I try and be considerate of the concerns of my teammates. In the past, we have agreed on a plan to communicate with each other so that it isn't just one person who carries the load. We share the responsibility out and ensure that we help each other. This creates a much happier less stressful working environment.

- I try and be proactive at working on any potential problems before they can become stressful. By doing this most of the time my work is kept controlled and doesn't become a source of stress to me. I focus on one thing at a time, prioritizing the most urgent tasks and those that can be resolved the quickest. That way I can stay on top of the situation.

Write your own answers here:

_____

_____

_____

_____

_____

_____

_____

_____

_____

_____

_____

_____

_____

_____

_____

Handling any kind of stress is about keeping it manageable. If you are well organized and plan your workload well and can make quick decisions when a problem arises then most of the time stress should be kept to a minimum. If you become overwhelmed, then ask team-mates for help. A company is only as strong as its parts, and if members of the company don't work well together, then it is likely there will be problems.

Another significant cause of stress is overthinking. If you are continually expecting the worse to happen, inevitably it will. Be positive in your outlook and visualize things working well for you. If you turn everything into a disaster in your mind, then it will turn into a disaster.

Many employers now recognize the benefits of stress relieving techniques such as visualization, deep breathing, meditation, and yoga. Some employers are even welcoming them into the workplace to help with employee wellbeing. If you find that your employer is an advocate of these strategies, then you can include them in your answers.

Similar Questions you Could be Asked

There are other ways this question may be asked, and these can include examples such as this:

- What aspect of your current job causes you the most stress?
- What strategies do you use to cope with stress?
- Tell me about something you found stressful in your previous job

Just remember to be positive in your answer and draw focus to your success and not your failure. Give good examples of the coping strategies you use and how they have proved to be effective in the past.

Reasons for the Question
Why should I hire you? This question is asked to find out why you think you are the best candidate for the role on offer. The employer has a specific position that requires filling and the person they chose to fill that job needs to be able to solve the problems it produces. You, therefore, need to be sure that you are confident and ready to complete all the necessary tasks as described in the job description.

How to Respond
First, write down each requirement listed in the job description. Next, to each point write down why you can fulfill the requirement including an example to demonstrate this.

Next, think beyond the requested qualities on the job description and consider what else would be advantageous to do the job well. Again, write down how you could facilitate this. You may have additional qualifications or experience that isn't required for the position but would be a definite asset. When you have made this note what qualities you can identify that run through as a theme, as these will be your greatest attributes for the job. Finally formulate an answer with examples to give at the interview, keeping it concise and to the point.

Answer Examples
- I have both the experience and qualifications detailed in your job description. My five years of working at X shows my dedication to the job. Over that time, I have built a strong rapport with customers and other team members, allowing me to move from the position of a sales team member to be the sales team manager. I believe that my expertise in this specialist field make me a good fit for the job
- Having carefully reviewed the requirements you listed necessary for the role of HR Manager I believe my

experience and the skills and qualifications I hold will make me an excellent fit for the position. I am a highly effective communicator, and I am used to dealing with the staff on a daily basis ensuring that their needs, as well as the companies, are met. My level of training far exceeds that required on the job description and combined with my excellent references I believe I could be a great asset to your organization.

- If you will permit me to demonstrate my skills and ability to you, I would be delighted. As you have seen on my resume, I possess all the necessary qualifications and experience you are looking for, and I feel a practical demonstration would allow you to see I am an excellent candidate.

- As we have discussed, you require a sales executive who can manage more than a dozen employees on their sales team. My ten years working as a sales manager has allowed me to develop excellent team-building strategies. I have won many awards for my role including Sales Manager of the Year on three separate occasions. If you decide to hire me, I can bring my award-winning skills to influence your sales team.

Write your own answers here:

Similar Questions you Could be Asked
Here are a few examples of similar questions.

- Why shouldn't we hire you?
- Why are you the best candidate for the job?
- What unique qualities can you bring to the job?

To answer the first of these questions "why shouldn't we hire you?" is not as you might think to be answered by saying something like "no reason at all, you should!" but rather by describing why they should, as an example:

- I cannot think of any reason not to hire me. I have all the qualifications, experience and skills you have requested. I am diligent, hardworking, reliable and autonomous. I work well as a member of a team and give my best effort to everything I do. I believe I would be a great asset to your company.

The other questions require the same approach I detailed earlier. It is necessary to match your abilities and experience to the job and exceed them where possible, then explain this concisely in your answer.

In Summary
Don't try and pretend you never experience stress or pressure, we all do. Instead focus on how you overcome it or make it work to your advantage.

When faced with a question about why you are the right candidate for a job ensure you know precisely what the job description required and that you not only meet but exceed those requirements.

CHAPTER EIGHT

What Are Your Hobbies and Interests?

What Are You Passionate About?

Although these questions may seem less serious than some of the others you will be asked during your interview, they still require the same careful though when answering. They may seem innocent enough but revealing anything that could be perceived by the employer to suggest your full focus may not be on the job could make the difference between getting the job offer or being passed by.

Reasons for the Question

Employers don't just want to know about your working background. They are also interested in finding out what makes you tick. This gives a better overview of you as a person and can reveal personality traits that may be advantageous or detrimental (in their opinion), to the job role they are offering.

By finding out what you like doing outside of work it can help them to build a better picture of you as an entire person and not just the face you wear during work hours. Some people are entirely different in their work environment compared to how they are in their leisure time.

Another reason for asking about your hobbies could be that the employer has concerns over your health or fitness or they might want to know if you are sociable and would be good working in a team or looking after clients.

The team you would be working with might have a certain chemistry that makes them gel well together, and the employer wants to find out if you would fit well into that team.

It is also a way of finding out where your true passions and motivations lie. If you are involved in dangerous sports, for example, they may feel that there is potential you could get injured and be unfit for work or would be unable to get jobs done correctly due to injury.

How to Respond

To answer this kind of question well, you should be honest and not try and make out that you do things just because you have done it once. For example, saying that you volunteer for a charity, doesn't mean that going to a couple of events organized by a charity each year make you a volunteer.

Employers are looking for people who are well-rounded in their interests and have the get-up and go to get involved with outside interests outside of work.

To prepare for this question make sure that you think about how you will answer in advance and remember that it should be about things you enjoy doing in your leisure time that won't interfere with your work time.

If you don't have a hobby as such, think about things you like doing when you finish work and what you do at the weekends. These might be activities you do with your family, friends or pets. Alternatively, they might be clubs you are part of, classes you go to, or associations you volunteer for.

When you finish compiling your list, think about the qualities the employer might be looking for to fulfill the job criteria. Try to learn about the company's culture and determine the sort of employee they could be looking for. Then see which activities on your list would demonstrate that you would be a good fit for the role.

Here is a list of hobbies that are good to tell employers about:

Daily Activities - Don't worry if you don't have any "hobbies," there will still be things you enjoy doing that you can mention; walking your dog, spending time with your children, reading, doing crossword puzzles, knitting, sewing, DIY. Think about what you do, even cooking dinner for your family, if you enjoy cooking, could be considered a pastime.

Keeping fit – If you go to the gym, swim, walk, run or do any kind of fitness classes, then they are great to mention. They demonstrate that you care about your health and wellbeing. Being involved with sports such as golf, tennis, squash or basketball demonstrate team playing and competitiveness that can be useful qualities in many jobs.

Adult Learning – The internet has provided us with a way to continue learning new things easily at home. There are many thousands of courses, lectures, seminars, and tutorials available online that can be done for pleasure or to further your career goals. There are plenty of other alternatives available too; your local community center may run courses or check out if anything is available through your local library. Learning need not be academic, you can literally learn anything! By choosing to pursue an education during your spare time, you are showing that you can be self-motivated, driven and ambitious.

Volunteering – If you are part of a community group or social project or help coach a children's sports team, then you are showing an employer that you care for others and not just about yourself.

Don't mention

Hobbies and interests that should perhaps be left unmentioned would include activities such as:
- Watching the TV
- Napping
- Gambling
- Partying
- Drinking

- Drug taking

Basically, avoid saying anything that can cast you in a negative light, even if you are only joking.

Employers will also generally prefer that their employees are not involved in dangerous sports such as race driving or fighting as the potential for injury is too great.

It is also best to tread carefully if your sport is highly competition based and requires that you go away a lot for games or tournaments.

An area that is either positive or negative is working in the services such as being a voluntary firefighter. Extreme respect and admiration must be given to those who put their lives on the line to help others, but regrettably, some employers might see it as too great a risk.

When possible try to make the hobbies, you choose to connect to the job you are being interviewed for. This will show that your interest in your career is more than about earning money and you value what you do. Also, focus on activities that demonstrate your best qualities that could be seen as a positive influence on your work. If for example, you work as a copywriter or editor, then talking about your passion for reading or writing your own novels could be advantageous.

When talking about your hobbies, ensure you also mention how they fit into your life. For example, you could be talking about how you enjoy running and that you start each day with a run that helps you to feel energized and ready for the workday ahead.

Tell the interviewer why you enjoy your passion so much and why it is so special to you. If you like to practice yoga, you could explain that you find it calming and that it helps keep your body feel strong and flexible.

Remember to keep what you say succinct and to the point. The interviewer won't want to hear your life history. That's why thinking about your answer carefully in advance and deciding what you will say is a good idea. You don't need to learn your answer like you would learn a script, just make sure you know what you are going to talk about and remember the points that link it to the job.

As I mentioned at the beginning, be honest and don't say things that aren't' true. It isn't going to be good if you get caught out from telling a lie! Also, if you aren't' being truthful, you won't be able to be reactive if the employer adds another question about your hobby. It could be that they have similar interests and they would see through any false information easily.

When your answers are genuine, and you genuinely enjoy what you do, then your answer will be interesting to listen to, animated and informative. It is vital that the employer feels you are enthusiastic and honest and have a positive outlook and this is an excellent area to show those qualities.

Answer Examples

Example answers for this question are trickier to give, as it is so dependent on your personality and the hobbies you have. As a very rough guide there are a few ideas here:

- I play a lot of sports, including soccer and hockey. I love being a member of the team and feeling the collaboration and team spirit. I am a social person, and team sport allows me to meet lots of new people.

- Ever since I was very young, I have loved to grow things in the garden. I have now become involved with a gardening project in my neighborhood, and I love sharing my passion with other children.

- I love everything to do with books. I enjoy reading in my spare time and before I go to bed. I find that I am transported into the story and can visualize what is going on. It is like visiting different worlds while never having to leave your own home. It helps me to look at the world with different eyes and appreciate what I have. I am currently working on writing my first novel.

Write your own answers here:

What Are You Passionate About? Is at first glance like the question on hobbies and interests. It differs in that it also encompasses your life passions, which could be more than just a hobby or interest and is about what is important in your life.

Reason for the Question
The reasons for asking about your passions are to discover what your values are and what kind of things interest you outside of the office. They could want to get to know more about you on a personal level so they can build a better rapport. They can also see if you will fit well into the company structure and culture. Although your passion need not be work-related, it will show a little of the type of person you are.

How to Respond
It shouldn't take much to work out what your passions are, unlike your hobbies and interests, passions are what you truly love, they could be your family, your pets, your home, garden, car, or about good causes that you back, such as reducing plastic waste, or planting trees. To be a passion it needs to be just the things you deeply care about.

It is quite likely that the interviewer will ask you follow up questions relating to your passion, so make sure it is something you can discuss easily and comfortably. Think about the kinds of follow up questions you might be asked so you have some idea how you will answer them.

If your passion has involved some level of training or reaching goals, then talk about this as it shows the interviewer how committed you can be and how you persevere to achieve your aims. Let the employer know what makes you so passionate about this activity and how it affects your daily life. This will give a good insight into the person you are.

An area to be cautious of is that it doesn't become apparent that your passion will interfere with your work. If an activity you are involved with takes up a lot of your time, then it might put employers off if they think you will be continually asking for leave. Try instead to focus the attention onto how your passions could potentially positively influence your work.

Answer Examples

As with the answers for hobbies and interests, answers about passions are highly personal to every individual, the answers given here show the kind of structure that can be used to answer the question.

- I am a passionate artist, and I love to paint. I have been studying art at night school and love to take my easel out and find beautiful locations to paint at the weekends. I find painting is a great way to relax and express my creative side. I can think about things differently when I am painting and often answers to problems just come to me.

- I love cooking for my family. I find the process of combining ingredients to create something almost magical highly satisfying. I have done several cookery courses in my spare time, and I am currently working on a cookbook. We often invite friends over on the weekend, and I love the social aspect of enjoying wonderful home cooked food together. It's also a great chance to swap recipes.

- I have a great passion for dogs and each morning before work I help at a special shelter where I help with the dog walking and grooming. On the weekends I help raise money for the charity that helps care for the dogs, by organizing fundraisers and fun activities for people to get involved in. Knowing that I am helping animals that can't help themselves makes me feel so good.

- My Mother is French, and I was brought up bilingual, and as a teenager, friends would ask me to help them improve their French. Over time I have ended up helping students on the weekends to speak French. I love doing it and seeing each student's abilities grow over time gives me huge amounts of pleasure.

Write your own answers here:

_____

_____

_____

_____

_____

_____

_____

_____

_____

_____

_____

_____

Conclusion

The answers you give to these questions are particular to everyone. What you should keep in mind is that your answers should reflect you in a good light. If possible, show skills that are transferable into the workplace and give the employer a better insight into who you are.

CHAPTER NINE

Questions About Your Education
Questions About Your Experience

For many jobs, your educational background and previous experience will make up an important part of your suitability for the job. Education doesn't stop when you leave college, many people go on to do further study outside of school as adult learners, and this type of study is often targeted to learning specific skills required for the career they want to peruse.

Reasons for the Question

The reason behind this question is apparent; the interviewer what's to know if your education and qualifications are enough for the job they are offering. Beyond this, they may also be interested to know about additional training you have taken of your own choosing as this shows many positive qualities.

The way the questions about your education are asked can take many different forms. The interviewer might say "Tell me about your education," or they may ask something specific such as "How did your educational background affect your career choices?"

They are interested in discovering how your education has prepared you for the job you are being interviewed for and if it meets the requirements that were specified in the job description.

If you don't have a strong academic background but still feel you meet the criteria of the job description, then be honest about it. It might be tempting to exaggerate the truth a bit, but it really isn't worth the risk as it will be simple for an employer to check your education credentials.

How to Respond

Be prepared to discuss both your major and your minor and any coursework that you completed. Think about how they relate to the job you're applying for and make sure your answers reflect this.

The employer may want to know why you chose the particular college you attended or course you did and what your long-term plan was at that time and if it has changed since you graduated.

You could also be asked about your GPA or your overall grades. Tell the truth and don't try to make excuses for yourself if they weren't as good as you would have liked.

Before you attend the interview write a list of the requirements detailed on the job description. Next, to each one write why you believe you fulfill the requirements. Don't forget about any projects you completed or courses you took that may have been instrumental in developing those skills. Another area to consider are any extracurricular activities that may have helped you gain the skills required for the job.

It could be that your educational background no longer reflects your career, but it is still worth thinking about skills that are transferable. For example, if you did an English major but now work as a copywriter, then the skills you learned in English are essential for good copywriting as you will know a lot about grammar and correct sentence structure.

If you did well in school don't play down your achievements, let employers know if you won any special awards or got high scores for projects and assignments.

Answer Samples

Many questions can be asked on this topic, so the answer samples are very generalized. If you follow the advice above, you should be able to answer any question put to you about your education with ease.

- My major was in English, which was great for developing excellent communication skills. However, I think that the extracurricular activities I was involved in were what really prepared me for the career I am now pursuing. I became president of the school's X association. This required me to organize fundraising events and galas to provide the association with the money it needed to succeed in its goals. The events I organized were always very well attended, and we continually exceeded our fund-raising goals. I was responsible for a team of 15 volunteers who helped me run the association and make it the success that it was. Because of this experience, I have learned how to be an effective manager and how to overcome obstacles and successfully run long-term projects.

- While I was studying for my degree, I realized that my true interests lay elsewhere so instead of completing the final year of my course I went to work with famine refugees in Somalia. Having worked in the field and seen firsthand the devastating effects such a disaster can have on a nation, I feel that I can now use my knowledge to work as an aid worker here in the United States.

- During the time I studied for my undergraduate degree I became skilled at computer coding. My interest drove me to learn Java, Python, PHP, and C# and I am now proficient in all of them. My skills in this area secured me a good job with an innovative tech company, but unfortunately, the business is being relocated, and although I have been offered the chance to go with them, I would prefer to remain living here. Currently, I am continuing with my studies by learning Ruby through an online course.

Write your own answers here:

Questions you Could be Asked
There are a great many questions you could be asked about your education, here are just a sample for you to consider.

- What reason did you have for choosing your major?
- What influenced you to choose your college?
- How has your education prepared you for this job/career?
- What activities were you involved in when you were at college?
- Did your career ideas change between starting and finishing college?
- What skills did you learn while at college that you can now apply in your chosen career?
- Were you happy with your final grades when you finished college?
- If you could have a college do over, would you choose the same course or something different? Why?

Just as with questions about your education, there are also many that can be asked about your experience.

Reasons for the Question
Employers want to gain a better understanding of your background and any previous work experience you may have. They are interested to know what experience will relate directly to the position they want to fill and if you have it. Your previous experience demonstrates your value to the company and whether you will be a good fit.

How to Respond
Begin by making a list of your experience, try to be detailed and include any additional training courses you completed or promotions you were given. Then look at the job description

and see how your experience matches it. It is more than just saying you have worked in customer services for three years, try to look more deeply for the skills you have acquired on the job and think about how they would be advantageous to the role you are being interviewed for.

Next, make sure the experience you will talk about at the interview ties in with the job description, so it is easy for the employer to see you have the right experience for the job.

To help make yourself stand out from the competition, think about experiences you have had where you were able to excel or solve a problem. This will help the employer see that you are conscientious and dedicated to your job.

If your old company had any incentivize earnings or rewards scheme, it could be a good way of demonstrating your skills. If for example, you were consistently the top seller each month or if you achieved more conversions than anyone else. Any kind of figures you can use as an example of your skills is a particularly persuasive tool.

Don't be tempted either to over embellish your previous job role or achievements as you could be found out when your references are checked. It is also an unwise choice as you may then be faced with a job you are incapable of doing, so it is better, to be honest.

Try to practice your responses, so you feel confident and relaxed when you are in the interview room. DO NOT try to memorize them as this will only cause you anxiety. As long as you have thought about what you should talk about and you emphasize the key point that makes you a good fit for the role you will be fine.

You should be able to give examples of why you would be proficient in all the skills that were detailed in the job description and not just one or two. By practicing you will be assured of your ability to answer the questions clearly and concisely and give quantifiable proof of your achievements, skills, and ethics. This will help you to stand out from the other candidates and give you a better chance of succeeding at getting the job.

Answer Examples

As there are many ways of asking you about your previous experience, you can use the examples below as a general guide on how to answer this type of question.

- Having worked as a customer services manager for three years, I have developed extensive skills and experience in the field. I am used to dealing with customer complains and have the ability to turn deescalate situations. I can quickly turn an irate customer into a happy one. Because the position was a management role, I oversaw a team of 20. Not only was I responsible for managing their daily duties, but I was also in charge of setting assignments and team training. Partway through last year, the company installed a new phone system that was more technologically advanced than the one we had before. I was sent on a two-day training course and was then required to teach the system to my team. Everything went very smoothly, and the changeover caused no problems.

- As a sales representative, I have gained two years of experience in the business to business sector selling specialist factory machinery. The company I was working for incentivized the sales team and set high targets. I was consistently the top of the incentivized sales list and always exceeded my monthly sales targets. This led me to be awarded salesman of the year, for which I was given a very generous bonus. I would expect to be able to bring the same level of expertise to this job as the product range is similar.

- I have been working part-time, evenings and weekends and during the school holidays, since I was 16. I come from a single parent family, and my Mom was bringing up three other kids so I wanted to help her in any way I could. I was awarded a scholarship to attend university and have now finished my degree. I am eager to give my Mom even more financial help.

- I have worked as an intern for a well-known firm in Atlanta. I was able to put that time towards my MBA, which I have recently completed. Now my family has moved here I am hoping that I will be able to secure a position with an equally reputable company and feel that the skills and experience I was given at X make me an excellent candidate for this junior role. I am very keen to learn and grow within the company.

Write your own answers here:

Questions you Could be Asked

These are just some examples of the questions you could be asked about your experience. Try practicing giving answers to each, and you will do fine in the interview.

- Why do you believe you have the right experience for the job?

- How will your previous experience help you in this job role?

- As you have no previous work experience, what other experience has helped prepare you for this role?

- How will the experience you have, make you a better choice for this position than other applicants?

Conclusion

It is impossible to tell precisely what questions you will be asked and how they will be phrased. By really thinking about the qualifications, skills, and experience you have, be that gained from the workplace or from other areas of your life, if you follow the suggestions given above and match your experience and qualifications to the job description with examples demonstrating your competence, then you will have no problems during the interview.

CHAPTER TEN
The Tough Interview Questions

Although you never know exactly what questions you will be asked during an interview, it is fair to say that some are easier to answer than others.

Some questions that can be tricky to answer can include questions about:

- Previous Bosses
- Supervisors
- Co-workers
- Working with others
- Your career goals

Previous Bosses, Supervisors and Co-workers

Probably one of the most awkward questions to answer is those about previous bosses, supervisors or co-workers, especially if you didn't get on with them. However, no matter how much you disliked them you absolutely cannot say so. Pay heed to the advice Thumper gave to his friend Bambi:

"If you can't say something nice, then don't say nothing at all" (Quote from the film Bambi).

Keeping negativity of any kind out of the interview is important. If you want to give yourself the best possible chance of being hired, then be positive. Negativity, defamatory comments, insults, and insinuations will raise a huge red flag that says to the employer, steer well clear of this one.

This doesn't mean you have to lie either; you merely have to word your responses to questions asked positively. Remember you may not realize that the person you didn't get along with is a friend of the interviewer, this wouldn't be uncommon if they are both working in the same industry.

Remember there are always two or more sides to every story. Differences of opinion are not uncommon in the workplace and professionally dealing with them is the right way to go about things.

It is OK to talk about differences of opinion if you don't bad mouth the other person. For example, you could explain how your team was divided over a certain issue and that after further brainstorming together, you successfully came upon a new idea you were all happy with. This shows co-operation, problem-solving and people skills.

If you left your previous job under a cloud, then it can be problematic to just leave a big hole in your resume by omitting the job entirely. It may also raise suspicion if you don't include your previous employer as a referee. In this instance, you could explain that there was a difference of opinion between yourself and your former boss or supervisor and that you have learned a lot from this. You realize that you should have been more open to communication and asking questions to reach a mutually agreeable outcome. You don't need to give specific details about the incident, just show that you learned from it.

Hopefully, there won't be any skeletons in your closet, and you will be able to talk favorably about the people you have worked with in the past. Employers are interested to know that you get along with people and are a team player.

If you do get asked a question that is tricky, don't just blurt out the first thing that comes into your head. Pause, consider your response and then reply.

Answer Examples

Q. Have you ever had to deal with a colleague who wasn't pulling their weight? If so, did you do anything about it and what was the outcome?

A. I worked in a very close-knit team, and a new member was brought in from another department to help us on a project because they had previous experience in that area. It quickly became apparent that this person was not actually contributing anything and was not being of any help to the team at all. During a break one afternoon I took them aside and politely asked them if there was a reason for this. It transpired that they were actually quite shy and had found it quite intimidating being asked to work with such a strong team, whom all knew each other so well. I brought the team together, and we all discussed the problem openly, welcoming the new person to our team and seeing what each of us could do individually to work with them. After that, we all pulled together to get the project done, and that person was a great asset.

Q. Have you ever had any conflict with someone in a higher position to you? If so, how did you resolve it?

A. Not long after I started my first job, I started having problems with the supervisor. She always seemed to be on my back hassling me over nothing. It was making me more and more unhappy, and I began not to want to go to work. Luckily another colleague told me that she always did this to the new recruits and that it wasn't that she was trying to be nasty, it was just her way of driving me to do my best. I decided to talk with the supervisor, and I explained to her honestly how she was making me feel and that rather than motivating me she was making me want to quit. The change in her attitude was astonishing; overnight she became supportive and appreciative when she could see I had worked hard. Her criticism and the almost aggressive approach she had had with me previously were gone completely. We went on to work exceptionally well together, and it was noticed that she never took that approach with another new employee again.

Q. Have you ever worked with someone you didn't like? How did you handle it?

A. I was the floor manager of a company that I had worked at for many years. When I went on maternity leave, I was replaced by a new woman who was employed to cover my leave. When I returned to the job she was retained, but in a lesser role. Her resentment towards me was apparent. She began to tell lies about me to my boss and was being incredibly nasty. Eventually I confronted her and asked her why she was doing this. She was highly embarrassed and denied that she had done anything. Other co-workers had also noticed her obvious dislike of me. I really didn't know what to do. I decided to talk to her again, this time with another colleague and again she denied it. A week later following another incident, I went to see my boss and explained the situation. The co-worker who had helped me talk to her was also asked what was going on and the woman was invited to attend a meeting between us all. She was clearly very uncomfortable, but as other co-workers were able to corroborate my story she was transferred to a different department. I would have preferred to be able to sort the situation between us amicably, but in this instance it just wasn't possible. I felt lucky that I had a team who supported me and was thankful for their help.

Write your own answers here:

Questions you Could be Asked

Here are a few more questions that you could be asked about your boss, supervisor or co-workers.

- Describe your perfect boss
- How would your boss describe you?
- What would you do if you knew your boss/supervisor/co-worker was wrong about something?
- What was the biggest criticism you have ever received at work?
- Have you ever misjudged someone at work? What did you do about it?
- How do you get along with colleagues who are older/younger than you?

People Skills and Working with Others

Employers want to hire people that are easy to get along with and even if you have the best resume, education, experience and qualifications you will lose out to someone whom the employer thinks will get along with people better. This is because conflicts in the workplace affect morale, take up time and can be challenging to resolve.

A stock response to a question about how you get on with others would be to say that you "like working with people." This gives no information to the interviewer about why you like working with people, or how you are easy to work with. Make sure that you provide examples to back up what you say

These are some people skills that are desirable:

- Listening and encouraging clients/co-workers to share their problems so a resolution can be found.
- Motivating team members and improving their performance.
- Leading team meetings and group discussions in a way that facilitates an easily drawn consensus.

- Develop strong relationships with customers by providing an outstanding level of customer care.
- Facilitate the successful mediation of conflicts
- Finding resolutions to customer complaints.

Give examples of actual situations where you have used these skills at work.

Answer Examples

Here are some example answers to the question "Do you work well with others?"

- My involvement in team projects has developed my communication abilities. It has also helped me learn how to mediate conflicts between other team members effectively. When members of my team have had difficulty in reaching an agreement, I ask them to tell me their concerns individually. These concerns are then shared with the group so we can all work on the right solution. This way the problems are shared and resolving them becomes easier.
- As a member of the customer care team, I am used to dealing with complaints and customer concerns. I am an excellent listener and allow them to tell me exactly what problems they are having. I empathize with their situation and then work with them to achieve a mutually beneficial resolution. My skills in this area have helped me to make the best customer satisfaction scores at my current company, and I was recently awarded customer representative of the year.

Write your own answers here:

Career Goals

Questions about your career goals can also be difficult to answer because it could be that you only want to use the job you are being interviewed for as a stepping stone to other things. Alternatively, it could be that you have no long-term plans for this job, but just need it to pay the bills until you can find something better/finish your studies/gain the qualifications you need for the career you really want and so on.

There are all kinds of reasons that you may only be looking for a job as a stop gap, but whatever they are it is usually best not to disclose this information to your potential new employer.

It could well be that you're looking to find a secure long-term job that can offer you the career advancement you desire, so landing the job is important to you.

When asked about your career goals the interviewer wants to know where you are heading and if you are looking for a long-term relationship with their company. They want to know if you will be a dedicated member of their team or just someone who is there for the money.

How to Respond

Focus first by working out what your short-term goals are and then progress to your long-term ones. Write them down and consider if the job you are applying for will help you to meet them. At this stage, you can include things like making money as this is one of your true aims, just not one you would say during an interview.

Once you have your goals written out write down HOW you will achieve them. For example, if you want to work as a manager write down the steps, you would need to take to accomplish this.

Ensure when you are writing down how you will achieve your goals, that you focus on the employer and mention that one of your goals includes working for their company. Draw attention on how reaching your goals will be of value to their business and that by them helping you reach your goals they will also achieve theirs.

Keep the goals general rather than very specific. If for example, your ambition is to run your own company, which would compete with theirs it should not be included in your response to their question.

Answer Examples

These are a few examples of answers you can use to create your own.

- In the first instance, I am hoping to achieve a position as a sales representative. I am excellent with people and enjoy providing exceptional customer service. I believe that working as a sales representative will allow me to develop my talents in this area further and I hope to become an area sales manager responsible for my team eventually.

- To begin with, I am looking to develop my communications and marketing skills. In the future, I am hoping that working for you will allow me to improve my abilities to a standard where I could be considered for a more senior role perhaps as a marketing manager. To help me achieve this I hope to have the opportunity to work as a team leader on projects, and by continuing with the training, I am doing online.

- Having just finished my training as a machine engineer, I am hoping that I can learn more specific skills working for your company. I am very keen to develop my abilities and continue my training with you so that I can eventually be a part of your international team.

Write your own answers here:

_____

_____

_____

_____

_____

_____

_____

_____

_____

_____

_____

_____

_____

_____

_____

Other Questions You Could be Asked

There are a few ways this type of question could be put to you. Here are some examples:

- If you were staying with your present employer, what would your next move be?
- What is your dream job and how would it help you achieve your career ambitions?
- What is your idea of the worst possible job for you?

In Summary

You can never be certain what questions you are going to be asked during a job interview. Remember to be honest, without being negative. Take time to think before you respond and prepare as much as possible before the day.

CHAPTER ELEVEN

Some Less Common Interview Questions

So far everything has been going great. You've researched the company well. You are confident that you exceed the requirements with your excellent work record, experience, and qualifications. You've managed to give great, informative well thought out answers to every question, and you are feeling quietly confident. You've started to relax and more at ease than when you entered the room, and you've managed to get some of the trickier questions out of the way you've discussed your strengths and explained why your weaknesses were a positive thing. You know you look great in your smart new suit, polished shoes and with your freshly trimmed hair.

Your interviewer smiles at you and rocking their pen between their fingers leans back and says, "Would you rather fight a mouse that was the size of a lion, or 100 lions that were the size of mice?"

The question flaws you, "where on earth did that come from" you think to yourself. You're left stammering like a fool "um, err, um" you mutter, while you frantically think what the right answer might be.

Of course, there is no right answer, it is a matter of preference, although I certainly know which I'd choose, and it wouldn't be the former.

Why do interviewers now seem to throw more of these seemingly random questions into their interviews? There are several reasons, which include trying to get behind the perfect employee veneer you have so carefully applied for your interview. Alternatively, it could be that they want to see what happens when they take you out of your comfort zone because of course, anything can happen when you are working on the job. Things are not always just black and white, often a whole rainbow of problems can dump themselves on your desk.

What you need to remember is that there is no right or wrong when it comes to answering these questions. Often the interviewer wants to hear a bit of originality, perhaps a little humor and see what you will do when faced with something you weren't expecting.

When you are answering these kinds of problems there are a couple of things you should keep in mind:

1. Try and keep your answer relevant to the job you are being interviewed for.
2. Explain the reasons behind your answer.

Incidentally, the reason for the question about the lion size mouse or the mice sized lions is to see if you prefer to tackle one big problem or lots of small ones at the same time.

It is almost standard practice in an interview not to get asked at least one question that seems rather bizarre. When this happens don't worry, below you will find some ideas that can help you overcome pretty much anything.

Keep Calm. If the interviewer asks you a question that you have no idea how to answer, don't panic. You can just say, "do you mind if I come back to that question, I will need time to think about it."

The reason most employers ask odd questions is to test your critical thinking skills. Most of the time there is no right or wrong answer to this type of question. One way of answering is by explaining your reasoning behind the answer as you give it. If you found the question, they asked confusing ask if they can clarify the meaning for you.

Preparation. One of the best ways to practice answering any questions you are asked is by asking a friend to act as the employer in a few "mock" interviews. By practicing your responses will start to come more easily and you won't feel as stressed when it comes to the actual interview. You can use the questions in this book or look online for lists of interview questions that are suitable for the type of job you are being interviewed for.

Keep the Focus on the Job. All the questions you are asked during the interview are used to ascertain if you are the right candidate for the job and see if you have the skill set that is required. Every answer you give should demonstrate your skills, qualifications and previous experience and prove to the employer that you have everything they are looking for and more.

If you get asked "What is your favorite color" you might answer "green because it is a calm color and I'm great at being calm under pressure."

A surprisingly common question at interview is "Tell me a joke." If you aren't a particularly "funny" individual, this can catch you by surprise. Recruiters are just seeing if you can think on your feet and if you have a good sense of humor. Making sure you do have a simple joke that is easy to remember prepared just in case it a great idea. It doesn't need to be anything complicated, in fact, the easier, the better, as you don't want to blow the punch line. Make sure the joke you pick is appropriate, suitable for all and inoffensive. Think of something you'd tell your Grandma.

Another more popular yet seemingly strange question at an interview is "What would you do if you won the lottery?" This is a bit of a character test, so don't rush your answer. Be honest – if you won the lottery would you stay working your job? It's generally unlikely. The employer wants to know what type of person you are if you would invest the money, donate some to charity, pay off your parents' mortgage, or blow the lot in Vegas.

A question that has become more frequently asked is "If you had a superpower, what would it be?" You have two choices here, you can be sincere and say which superpower you would most like to have, or you could tailor your answer to fit the job you are applying for. No answer is wrong in this situation.

Another example of a character and resourcefulness test is the question "If there was an apocalypse would you survive? How?" We've all seen disaster movies, and you could use that as part of your answer. If you do have actual survival skills, then go right ahead and let them know. A good answer would be to talk about building a team so you could work together and utilize each other's strengths.

More unusual questions

1. "If you were an animal, what animal would you be?"

This is asked to determine more about your characteristics. For example:

- Monkey = clever, agile and mischievous, lives in social groups.
- Elephant = strong, wise and kind and a member of a herd with hierarchy.
- Horse = fast, powerful, high spirited and a member of a herd with a hierarchy.
- Dog = friendly, loyal, protective.
- Cat = aloof, agile, loner.

Think about the qualities needed for the job and pick your animal appropriately to reflect them, explain your reason for choosing the animal.

2. "Do you believe in fairies?"

This question like this is asked to see if you will fit into a team. There isn't a right or wrong answer, but the interviewer is looking for you to inject perhaps a little humor and to relate your answer to the job you are being interviewed for.

3. "If you had a stapler with no staples, what else would you use it for?"

A question such as this is looking to see if you can think outside of the box. It is highly likely that many people will give the same or a similar answer, the two most common are "nothing, I'd throw it away" or "a paperweight." Try here to think outside the box, be a little inventive and say something different that will separate you from the rest of the interviewees.

4. "Why are manhole covers round?"

Is another way of finding out how creative you are?

You don't actually need to give a reason; you could say something like "why are roses red? Why are violets blue? I'm sure I don't know, do you?" Again, you are looking to say something that is memorable and a little bit clever. Simply answering "I don't know" really isn't going to cut it.

5. "How many times a day do a working clocks hour and minute hands overlap?"

The answer here is actually 22, but this isn't really what the interviewer is trying to find out. What they really know is how you go about solving problems. You could answer the question by saying "let me work it out" while you doodle on a piece of paper, or if you did already know the answer you could say "ahh I happen to know that it is 22, but if I didn't know I would work it out for you".

6. "When placed in boiling water and heated further, the hotdog splits. In which direction does it split and why is this?"

There is obviously a correct scientific answer to this question, but as you aren't going to able to do the experiment to find out the real answer, you can only speculate. What the interviewer is interested in learning about you here is your reasoning skills. How will you formulate your response? Be sure to explain your thought processes as you answer and remember it isn't about being right or wrong, it's about how you get there.

7. "What would be the title of your first novel and what would it be about?"

This is a look at your deeper personality and also possibly your work ethic. Try to choose something that draws some relevance to the company or job and try to make it memorable and interesting. You can again walk the interviewer through your thought processes.

8. "You're the boss. You wake up at 3 a.m. with a feeling that something is wrong at work, what do you do?"

A question such as this is looking at how you would respond when you are in a position of responsibility. It is quite likely that the interviewer will follow up this question with "You're the lowest paid employee in the company. You wake up at 3 am with a feeling that something is wrong at work, what do you do?" I probably don't need to spell this out for you, but obviously, you need to act whether you are the boss or the downtrodden employee. The question is trying to work out if you are a responsible individual who cares about their job.

9. "How would you sell ice cream in Alaska?"

Your creativity and problem solving, think outside of the box qualities are being put to the test with this question. Believe it or not, it can get warm in Alaska, so I would probably concentrate my answer on researching that and look at hotels and restaurants that might want to incorporate ice cream into their dessert menus.

10. "If you were given $50,000 to start your own business, what kind of business would it be?"

This question is just looking at your common sense and if you would follow a path that supports what you put on your resume. If you go entirely off-piste here and say you'd start a casino, when you are a welder, the employer might wonder if you do actually have any common sense. Always try to bring the question back to reflect the job you are being interviewed for.

11. "If I handed you a $1000 and told you to double it in 24 hours, how would you do it?"

To test your problem solving, creativity and think outside of the box mental attitude, this kind of question gives you a choice, would you take a risk and gamble to win, or would you make a sound investment in something that was hard to lose?

12. "If you started your own brand, what would the brand motto be?"

This type of question can be tough to answer as I know it would take me days to come up with a motto for any brand I was creating. Whet the employer is looking for here is something that shows your work ethic and to see how quickly you can think when you are put on the spot.

13. "It's a hot day, and you want to go for a swim, but as you are about to dive in the pool, you see there is an alligator. What do you do?"

This is another problem-solving skills question. Hopefully, you wouldn't say that you'd try to get it out in any way and would, in fact, call in the professionals. There is a time for heroics and a time to be sensible.

14. "How many people make a crowd?"

There is no agreed figure to answer this question, so it is a matter of perspective. The interviewer is really interested in understanding your reasoning when trying to come up with an answer and to see if it would take a lot or only a few people before you considered it a crowd.

Write your own answers here;

_____

_____

_____

_____

_____

_____

_____

_____

_____

_____

_____

In Summary
The trick when answering any more unusual questions is to:

- Stay calm
- Take your time
- Voice your thinking and not just your answer
- Give full answers
- Don't just say you don't know the answer
- If you really can't answer the question, ask for more time or to come back to the questions later when you've had more chance to think about it.

CHAPTER TWELVE

How to Handle Inappropriate or Illegal Interview Questions

There are topics where interviewers shouldn't dare to tread. Unfortunately, however, this isn't always what happens. Questions relating to your gender, age, religion, family, citizenship, disability or criminal record are a few areas that are not to be asked about.

Only questions that directly ascertain if you are a suitable candidate for the job should be asked, and although elements of the areas mentioned above could constitute reasonable proof of this, they are still not acceptable in an interview.

There are very few exceptions, and this is only in circumstances where the employee must meet particular criteria. For example, a job in a woman's refuge would only be open to women. A job for an employee working in a liquor store can justifiably exclude an applicant who is below the legal age to sell liquor.

How to Respond

If you are asked a question that you believe is illegal and could be used to discriminate against you getting the job, you can justifiably refuse to answer the question. It may feel embarrassing, but you need not make a big deal over it. Simply say, "I do not wish to answer that question" and move on. If the employer asks you why you can tell them that questions about "X" are considered discriminatory and are against federal law.

If an interviewer asks you an inappropriate question by accident, and you can see there is no malice intended in what they ask you can avoid answering the direct question, but instead give them an answer that addresses the substance of the question.

Age

As in the example given above when the job applicant needed to be old enough to work in a liquor store, other jobs would also apply in this area such as bartender casino floor worker and so on. In these circumstances, an employer can ask to see the documentation that shows proof of age, but they cannot directly ask the questions:

- How old are you?
- What year were your born?
- When did you graduate?

If asked these questions you can give no answer, or you could say "my age has no bearing on my suitability for this job".

Gender

The question of gender and sexuality is another area of taboo. The only circumstances in which your gender can have any bearing on your suitability for the job is when the job can only be done by a person of a particular gender. For example, if you were applying for a job in a women's refuge or as an attendant for a restroom that is gender-specific.

Race

Direct questions about your ethnic background are illegal, but an employer can ask you questions about the number of languages you are fluent in the ability to speak more than one language is part of the job role. They can also legally ask if you are legally eligible to work in the US.

Finances

You cannot be asked about your credit rating, financial status or about any debt you hold in an interview. The only exceptions to this could be specific requirements that have to be met if you were, for instance, applying for a job in a bank. It is also legal for employers to run a credit check on job applicants, but only with the applicant's permission.

Disability

Equal opportunities for all make it very clear that unless a person's disability would prevent them from performing the tasks required for the job, they are applying for then any limitations they have, may not be used to discriminate against them. An employer cannot ask you direct questions about your disability, but they can ask questions that pertain to the requirements of the job. For instance, if you were applying to work in a warehouse a reasonable question to ask would be "Can you lift and move products that weigh in excess of 35 pounds?" for example.

A potential employer cannot ask you anything to do with your weight, height, mental or physical health unless it directly relates to the job and forms part of the job requirements. If you do get asked such a question, you can reply that you feel confident in your ability to do the job.

The ADA (Americans with Disabilities Act) gives protection to job seekers who have disabilities. Employers cannot discriminate against an applicant with a disability who is qualified for the role being offered.

Family

You cannot be asked about your marital status, if you have children, if you intend to have children, childcare arrangements or anything about your spouse. These are all your personal information that does not need to be disclosed to an employer.

Interviewers can use questions that ask about your ability to travel, attend out of hours meetings, or about the length of time you anticipate you will stay in a job. You can also be asked in you can foresee any reasons why you might need extended leave.

Criminal Record

Employers have the right to ask about any crimes for which you have been convicted if it has a direct relation to the job duties you will be carrying out.

For example, if you will be handling merchandise or dealing with any form of money transaction be it online or in the physical environment, you can be asked if you have any convictions for theft or money laundering.

You cannot be asked if you have ever been arrested, if you have been involved in any form of demonstrations or if you have any strong political views.

It is possible in some states for an employer to check your criminal background.

Religious Beliefs

You cannot be asked about your religious beliefs or religious holidays you observe. However, you can be asked if there are any reasons why you cannot work during the company's regular business hours.

If you are asked questions regarding your religion, you can refuse to respond, or you can say that your faith will not affect your ability to carry out the job.

Filing a Discrimination Claim

If you feel you were discriminated against during an interview, then you are entitled to make a claim for discrimination. It is worth considering however that in many cases the interviewer probably wasn't trying to be discriminatory. Often employers are not aware of the law and do not realize that questions of this type are not allowed. By filing a case against a company, there is a possibility that news will get around and then no employer will employ you because they see you as a trouble maker.

In Summary

If you think an employer is asking you a question that is illegal or discriminatory don't overreact. You have four choices:

- You can answer the question
- You can say you do not wish to answer the question
- You can state that whatever the question was about (your age, your gender, your family, your religion and so on) will not affect your ability to do the job
- You can answer the question in a modified way so that it doesn't involve the part that touched on the illegal or discriminatory topic.

If you do genuinely feel that you were unfairly discriminated against in an interview, you can file a discrimination claim.

CHAPTER THIRTEEN

What Are Your Salary Expectations?

Have You Any Questions to Ask Me?

The tricky subject of salary negotiations often can feel somewhat awkward. What if they offer you less than you were expecting? How much should you ask for? We will look at ways of resolving these issues.

When you are asked if you have any questions, it is easy to become tongue-tied and then kick yourself later when you think of half a dozen things you needed to know.

In truth neither of these questions has to be difficult at all, providing you do your homework.

Reasons for the Question

The reason employers ask you about your salary expectation is that they want to know if they can afford you.

Sometimes employers can be bargain hunting, looking for employees who are willing to work for a lower amount than the current market rate. It is vital that you don't fall foul of this and ensure that you highlight why you are of value and worth the salary for which you are asking.

Another reason for the question is employers want to see what value you put upon yourself and if you are confident enough to request the amount you deserve or will merely accept any offer given. If your salary expectations are way above the industry norms, they would need to know what makes you so extra special and why they should spend that amount of money employing you. If you undervalue yourself, they may wonder why you have such little regard for the value of your work. This question can certainly tell a lot about someone's character, if you are overconfident and full of your self-worth or if you are timid and shy and feel you are worthless.

During salary negotiations, your aim is to convince the potential employer of your worth to their business. You should do this before you enter into any salary negotiations.

How to Respond

While you don't want to undervalue yourself as if the employer then offers you a lesser amount you could end up out of pocket. You also don't want to make your aims too high. Your expectations will need to be in line with the company's salary range.

It can be difficult to judge what salary you should ask for before the interview, as you still don't know the finer details of what your role will be. It is common practice for employers to include in the job application form a question asking about your salary range requirements.

If you have come from a similar job role, then you may already be aware of the market norms when it comes to salary, but if the job is new to you, then you will need to do some research. Start by looking at the salary amounts being offered for similar positions and make a note of the lowest and highest figures. Try to find others working in the same field and ask them what they would consider a reasonable salary at your level. There are also websites that can give you a guide about salary averages, so try looking on Indeed.com, Salary.com or Payscale.com for ideas. Try to look at as many sources as you can to get an accurate idea.

Remember that certain variables will also alter the salaries being offered. If you will be working in New York, then the pay will be a lot higher than if you are going to be working in a small town in the central USA. If you are changing jobs because you are moving state remember that the cost of living can vary, and you may need to be adaptable. It is unlikely that small-town employers will be able to compete with the salaries given by large city companies.

Once you have established an acceptable salary range, that applies to where you live, you can discuss the matter from the point of authority, rather than just stabbing about in the dark. Hopefully, the employer will be a fair one and will know the current acceptable rates for the job you are applying for, so you shouldn't be too far out of the ballpark.

Changing jobs is the perfect time to give yourself a raise. If you believe you are worth extra money due to your experience and qualifications, then it is reasonable to add between 10 to 20 percent on to what you are currently being paid, providing it is still within the range of pay acceptable for your job role and your level of experience.

It can sometimes be tempting to grab any offer you are given, mainly when jobs are scarce. However, if the amount you are offered is too low, don't sell yourself short. Explain why you believe you are worth more and that you have researched the market and ask for what you want. If you settle for less, you will end up regretting it. Your job should pay you enough to live on without struggling.

When you are filling in job applications put in a salary range rather than a fixed sum. Make the lower figure very close to what you would be looking to achieve and the higher figure above this. If you only put a single number in, it may seem that you are not negotiable about your salary requirements.

Answer Examples

- Due to my experience and qualifications, I am expecting a salary of between $X and $Y.

- I am flexible about my salary range and open to discussion on specifics when the full details about the job role have been revealed.

- Because I have only recently moved to this area, I took the trouble to research the correct salary levels here. For the position, you are offering, and in line with my level of experience, I believe that my salary should be between $X and $Y.

- I would like to know more about the job role before discussing my salary expectations.

- I am flexible about my salary requirements and believe my extensive experience, and excellent credentials will add value to my candidacy. When we have discussed in detail the responsibilities of the role, I will be happy to offer you my salary expectations.

- Based on my previous salary for a similar job role, I believe that a fair expectation would be between $X and $Y. This takes into account the current figures payable in the industry and the geographical location. I am happy to discuss this with you.

Write your own answers here:

Similar Questions You Could be Asked

There are other ways that the same question could be put to you. However, it is voiced, your responses will still be based on your research and the value, you believe you have to the job.

- How much are you looking to make?
- What is your current salary?
- How much do you believe you are worth to my company?
- Would a salary of $X be of interest to you?

However, this type of question is put to you be calm and promote your strengths. Be true to your expectations and your needs. If the salary being offered is insufficient for your requirements be honest and say so. If they are unwilling to negotiate further, then it will probably be better for you to look for a different job that can match your requirements.

The question, "Have you any questions to ask me," usually comes at the end of the interview and you want to ensure that you have well-constructed, valuable questions to ask. To do this takes a little thought about what you want to know, and you should write your list of questions down. During the interview, it is quite likely that some of the questions will be answered and if possible, you should note down the answers next to the questions as you go. By the end of the interview only some of your questions will remain and these you can put forward to the interviewer.

Reason for the Question

Employers ask this question because they genuinely want to know if you have any questions about the job role or the company. No surprises there then. They are also curious to see what you will ask, will they be valuable, relevant questions about the workings of their company, or will they be silly questions that don't really affect the job you are applying for? Hopefully, you will stick with the former as you don't want the interviewer to think you haven't adequately prepared and are therefore not really interested in the job. Asking the right questions is important as it is your opportunity to ensure that it is the right job for you.

How to Respond

How many questions should you ask? This can be tricky as it depends on what information has been omitted during the interview. You can ask questions during the interview process if you are discussing a topic and need a point clarifying. Generally speaking, you should ask between two and five questions to demonstrate you are interested in the business and the job. It also indicates that you have made an effort to do some homework and wanted to find out more about the company.

When preparing your questions try to aim for between 8 to 10 as some will be answered naturally during the process of the interview. If you still have more than five remaining at the end of the interview, select the best from those you have left and leave the rest.

When preparing your questions, ensure that they are well phrased, comprehensive and target the exact information you want. This isn't the time to be ambiguous. Also, make sure that the questions are open-ended and not closed questions.

An open-ended question if you are unsure, is one that requires the responder to give a full sentence reply and not just a simple yes or no answer. An example of an open-ended question would be "How frequently do you offer staff training?" as the interviewer needs to give a full answer. The similar question asked as a closed question would be" Do you offer staff training?" where the interviewer could simply answer "yes" or "no." One way to ensure your questions are open-ended is to use action words to start them, these include:

- What
- How
- Who
- Where
- When
- Describe

Using these types of words to start your questions sentences will help to ensure they are open-ended.

What sort of questions should you ask? This is difficult to answer as it will depend on the job you are being interviewed for. Some standard questions include:

1. "Please, could you describe the day-to-day responsibilities of the job?"
    This question allows you to learn the details of the job role, allowing you to decide if it is right for you. It will also help you to gain insights about the skills, strengths, and responsibilities and discuss any topics it brings up that have not been covered in the interview.

2. "What essential qualities are you looking for in the person to fill this role?"
    This question lets you know exactly what the employer is looking for and if you fit the criteria.

3. "What qualities would you deem necessary for someone to excel in this job?"
    By asking this, you will find out more about the job and the expectations of the employer, helping you to see if you will be a good fit.

4. "What does the Company hope to achieve over the next five years?"

Hopefully, the response to this question will help you determine if the company is growing and that your job is likely to be secure.

5. "Who are your main competitors and how does your company stand out from them?"

   If you have researched the company well then you should have a good idea about the company's competitors already, but by asking them how they stand out from the competition will make the interviewer reveal more about the companies strategies to succeed in the marketplace and let you know if their future aims are in line with your own.

6. "What opportunities are available to staff; can they grow within the company?"

   This question finds out if the company is dedicated to training and working with their staff, or if they tend to recruit from outside to fill any roles that become available at higher levels.

7. "Can you tell me what challenges the company is currently facing and how you plan to overcome them?"

   This can be awkward for an employer to answer, they may not want to admit that there is anything causing concern. It is a great question to gauge if an employer is truthful and upfront with their staff. It also helps you to understand problems that may be facing the entire industry and see how your skills might help the business to overcome them.

8. "What's the best thing about working for this company?"

   This can give you an insight into the culture within the company and see if the company is supportive of its staff.

9. "What career path could I expect if I am offered this job?"
   It is important to know what prospect you may have within the company and how career advancement works there. It shows the interviewer that you aren't just looking to stay at the entry level but want to advance your career with them.

10. "What would you say is the toughest part of the job?"
    By asking this question, you should be able to find out if any particular pressures can be difficult.

11. "What superpowers would be useful in this role?"
    This is a fun question to ask if you have been given a few "out there" questions during the interview.

12. "Would you keep working here if you won the lottery?"
A true test of just how great the company is to work for.

Remember to be professional and avoid asking questions such as "How fast could I get a promotion?" or "Do you check references?" Think carefully about the questions you ask and how they will make you look to the employer.

Write your own answers here:

_____

_____

_____

_____

_____

In Summary

Make sure you research the company thoroughly in advance, so you know exactly what they do.

Don't be afraid to ask questions throughout the interview if you need further clarification on something.

Prepare your list of questions in advance and check them off when they get answered during the interview process.

By the end of the interview ask two to five questions.

Make sure all questions you ask are open-ended, so you get full answers.

CHAPTER FOURTEEN
More Than Just Answering Questions

In this chapter, we are going to look at what an interviewer is looking at besides the answers you give to their questions. This includes how you come across, are you outgoing or introvert, confident of nervous, a go-getter or a make doer. Also, how you appear, how you speak, how you make the interviewer feel. All these things and more, can either get you hired or interview expired.

First impressions count! You only get one chance to make a good first impression, so make sure it counts.

1. Cleanliness. It may seem obvious, but you don't want to go into an interview room stinking. Yes, body odor is natural, but you don't need to share yours with other people. Ensure that you are clean and fresh, have applied a suitable deodorant and that the clothes you are wearing are freshly laundered.

   In the summer months it can sometimes be challenging to remove body odor from clothing, a bacteria buildup causes this, they love warm damp conditions and washing alone isn't enough to kill the bacteria, so as soon as they warm up the odor is rereleased. To kill bacteria on your clothes, you can buy antibacterial detergents to add to your washing machine, or you can simply replace your fabric softener with a cup of white vinegar. This kills bacteria and leaves clothes smelling fresh, don't worry, they won't smell like vinegar. White vinegar is a much healthier product to use than fabric softener, and it won't damage your clothes as fabric softener can, so it is a worthwhile swap.

2. Clothing. If you are being interviewed for an office job, then it is always appropriate to wear a suit including jacket and tie for men. If the job is for a position in a different working environment such as a factory, workshop or outside job, then appropriate clothing can be worn. If you will be expected to demonstrate your skills as part of the interview if you were a welder for example, then wearing or at least taking appropriate overalls and safety equipment with you would be a good idea.

   Regardless of what you do wear to the interview ensure it is clean and tidy. Iron it or get it professionally laundered and pressed.

   Ensure your shoes are clean and polished and you are wearing matching socks.

   If you can't afford a suit for a job interview then try visiting your local thrift stores and tell them what you need, they will be only too pleased to help you out and you can often find very nice clothes for just a few dollars.

3. Hair and Nails. Make sure your hair is tidy and looks well kept. Going to an interview looking like a scarecrow won't get you remembered for the right reasons. Make sure too that your fingernails are clean and looking good. Dirty fingernails show that you don't care about your appearance and it could indicate to an employer that you wouldn't care much about your job either.

4. Positive Attitude. Ensure you enter the interview with a positive mental attitude. If you are enthusiastic,

optimistic, genuine and seem to be a bright and honest person you stand a far greater chance of being offered the position than someone who is negative, pessimistic, bitter, dower and would seem like they will bring the rest of the team down.

5. Problem Solver. Show that you are a great problem solver and are good at finding solutions to issues that arise. Swiftly implementing solutions to problems can be highly advantageous.

6. Fast Learner. Demonstrate your ability to learn new things quickly and to implement your new skills on the job. Having the ability to acclimatize yourself rapidly to a new work environment and cause the minimum amount of disruption to other employees is a skill that is well prized by employers.

7. Flexibility. The ability to be flexible and not stick rigidly to a method of doing things can be advantageous in a new work environment. Sometimes by being flexible, you will learn new skills and new ways of doing things that you weren't aware of before. Say to your interviewer that you are flexible about things.

8. Communication. Having the ability to communicate well is a crucial skill in any organization. It is the difference between having a team who work seamlessly together and a team that doesn't have a clue what is going on. You should be able to demonstrate that you have excellent communication skills in different aspects of your job, from talking to customers to keeping colleagues informed on the progress being made on projects. An easy exchange of information is essential to good business.

9. Collaboration. Show that you are good at collaborating with team members and can openly share your views, thoughts, and ideas. Also, show that even when the team can't agree that measures can be taken to find a solution by using collaboration. It is essential that you have good collaboration skills and are open to listening to other people's ideas if you are going to fit well into a team working environment.

10. Psychology. Before attending your interview, it is essential to prepare yourself psychologically for it. Get friends or family to help you do mock interviews or at the very least try interviewing yourself in the mirror. You may feel silly, but this is a great way to get over the embarrassment and make yourself feel far more confident once you enter the interview room.

    When the day of the interview arrives, make sure you give yourself enough time to prepare yourself. Don't leave anything to the last minute; you want to come feeling fresh, confident and well prepared and not hot, sweaty, nervous, rushed and unprepared. Avoid any form of stimulant before the interview, no coffee, chocolate or energy drinks for example. You need to be calm and relaxed. You can try listening to calming music that can reduce anxiety and help you feel at ease. There are lots of examples available on YouTube, try some that utilize frequencies to stimulate concentration and remove negative energy. If you practice meditation, then meditate to prepare yourself before the interview. If not, you can try breathing techniques that can help to make you calm.

11. Food. Even though you may not feel like eating, it is a good idea to ensure you have eaten a decent meal

before your interview as this will help to stabilize your blood sugar and avoid any embarrassing tummy rumblings.

12. Revise. Before you enter the interview building re-read your resume and your cover letter and any notes you have written to ensure you feel confident that the information you need is fresh in your mind.

13. Time. Don't leave making the journey to the place of your interview too late. You don't want to feel rushed so allow plenty of time that will allow time in case there are any holdups along the way. It is always better to arrive a little early than a little late.

14. Interview them. Remember that it isn't just the interviewer interviewing you for the job, it is also you interviewing them to see if you want their job. Something that appears excellent in a job advert could turn out to be something completely different when you find out all the facts. By taking on the attitude that you are interviewing them, it will help you to feel stronger and more in control. Don't be afraid to ask questions along the way, or if you are asked not to ask questions through the interview, write them down so you can ask them at the end.

Sometimes you will read about a job that really appeals to you, but you don't have all the qualifications or experience that is detailed in the job description. This doesn't necessarily mean you shouldn't apply for the job. It just means you will need to work harder and shine extra brightly during the interview.

It is often the case that employers will include in their job requirements, elements that they would like, but that are not actually essential to do the job in question. Some job requirements will always be more essential than others. It is therefore not uncommon for them to interview candidates that don't have all the requirements made in the job description if the candidates excel in the essential skills areas.

The more closely matched with their ideal candidate the more chance you have of getting interviewed. If you make it through to the interview stage, then it is reasonable to think that they must at least on paper feel you would be suitable for the job. It is just a matter of strengthening this belief during your interview.

In Summary

Regardless of the job, you are being interviewed for preparation is the key to success. By ensuring you are:

- Clean
- Tidy
- Well dressed
- Have done the necessary homework to be able to answer all questions fully
- Have practiced mock interviews
- Being positive
- Staying calm
- Getting to the interview slightly early

If you do these things, you should have no problems with completing a successful interview.

Before moving on to the conclusion, I would like to ask you, if you could go to Amazon and leave a review of the book so that other people can find it more easily. Reviews are the lifeblood of my book, and I would much appreciate it if you could do me this favor.
Now to the conclusion.

CONCLUSION

As you have seen through this book, the ability to ace an interview is something of a science or an art. It requires proper preparation, confidence and the ability to show an employer that you indeed are the best candidate for the role.

A good tip is to remember that if the interviewer is unused to giving interviews that often, they can be just as nervous as you are. Interviewing well is a skill, just as much as giving a good interview.

To recap let's look at how to give a great interview.

Preparation

Don't ever think it's worth not putting in the effort to do some proper preparation before an interview, no matter how many times you have been interviewed before. You interviewer will be able to tell that you haven't done the research necessary to give full strong answers to their questions.

You should find out all you can about the company and its background, its working practices, mission statement, ethics, and history. If possible, try to talk to other people who work there to give you a bit of insider knowledge.

You also need to pay close attention to the job description and ensure that your qualifications, skills and experience match or at the very least come close to those detailed. When formulating ideas for responses to the most common questions remember always to make your answers reflective of the job description, so it can be clearly seen that you are suitable for the role. This will also help you answer the more unusual questions that you can't really prepare for.

Practice

Make sure that you practice answering questions in a few mock interviews. You can do this by asking friends or family to interview you or by using mock interviews online or by merely interviewing yourself in a mirror. It may sound silly, but it works to make you feel comfortable and get over the embarrassment.

Practice does indeed make perfect, and it is well worth taking the time and effort to do this.

Punctuality

Make sure that you arrive at the place of your interview ten to fifteen minutes before your allotted interview time. Arriving late to an interview is just like telling the interviewer "Heck, I don't care at all about this job, you go right on ahead and give it to someone else."

To ensure that you do arrive on time plan your day and your journey carefully and allow for any holdups, you might encounter.

Listen, THINK, Answer

When you're nervous, it can be easy just to blurt out the first thing that comes into your head. Resist the temptation to do that! Always think before you answer a question and if your thinking time needs more than a few seconds to say, "would you mind if a take a moment to think about that?" They aren't going to say "no." Of course, you can't sit there is total silence for the next 10 minutes either, so if you can't think of an answer ask if they'd mind if you came back to the question later.

Try to avoid putting in sounds before you answer such as "um" or "err." If you want to buy thinking time, try repeating the question back to the interviewer or say something like "That's an interesting question."

Be Audible

When you are nervous, it can do strange things to the way you speak. Either you may speak so quickly that the interviewer can't understand you, or so quietly they can't hear you. Take a breath, speak at a regular speed and speak clearly at a reasonable volume, so they aren't straining to hear what you say. Make sure you look at your interviewer or across the panel if there is more than one while you are speaking, don't look down at the floor, or play with your clothing.

Don't Fidget

Many people when they are under pressure do things entirely subconsciously. They fiddle with their hands, move around in their chair, regularly clear their throat, the list goes on. When you are being interviewed these are all signs of stress and discomfort. You want to exude confidence and professionalism so sit in the chair comfortable, sit up, don't slouch, put your hands in your lap and smile at your interviewer. Every so often think about how you are sitting and if you are doing anything fidgety.

Confidence, Not Arrogance

Giving an air of confidence in your interview is essential. You want the employer to think you are a capable person, who they will be able to trust and rely upon. However, this is very different from being arrogant. It doesn't matter if you think you are the best person in the world for the job if you are the best trained, most experienced, highest qualified if you are full of your own self-importance are arrogant or narcissistic, then you are not a team player. You will cause problems with your co-workers and possibly even with your clients, and you will not be given the job.

Show that you are a team player and you can listen to and act upon other people's opinions. That you appreciate your co-workers and are humble about your success.

Be Attentive, Listen

When you first enter the interview room, your heart is racing, your mind is darting from one thought to another, or you feel like you can't think at all. As you are asked the first few questions, you begin to calm down and feel more at ease. As the adrenalin subsides a strange phenomenon can occur, and you can find yourself zoning out and no longer listening carefully to what the interviewer is saying to you. It is essential that you do listen carefully to everything the interviewer says as you might completely miss the point of a question they are asking, which will cause you to answer it incorrectly. Be sure you remain present and don't allow yourself to zone out.

Positive Mental Attitude

People who are pessimistic and are always spouting doom and gloom are the worst. They make you feel low, they can extinguish your optimism in a matter of moments, and they just drone on and on all doom and gloom. In an interview, a person like this will destroy any chance they have of getting the job. Their negativity quickly alerts the interviewer that this person would be a disaster in a team and no matter how good their qualifications or experience might be, they aren't' worth taking the risk on.

If you come into an interview with a bad attitude, badmouthing your last boss or co-workers, then the employer will quite rightly not consider you for the job.

It isn't just what negative people say either; their body language can also be a big tell. Crossing your arms and legs and slouching in the seat is immediately a very negative signal to an interviewer. Try to sit comfortably but upright with your hands one on top of the other in your lap.

Smile

It is a simple enough thing to say smile, but a smile is such an important thing. You don't need to grin throughout the interview like the Cheshire cat, but a genuinely friendly smile maintained throughout the interview will not only lift your own spirits it will also make you more likable to the employer. Someone who is smiling seems more approachable, more connected and sincere.

Be Interested Not Desperate

Rather like a first date if you show you appear to your interviewer to be disinterested, distracted, apathetic and dull, then you won't be getting the job, just like you wouldn't get a second date. Equally being overly keen is just as off-putting. It may well be that you really do need to get the job but appearing desperate by pleasing and begging will not get it for you.

Show interest in the job and the company and show the interviewer that you have a passion for the role they are offering.

Mind Your Manners

Being polite and saying "hello" and "thank you" is not optional. It is essential if you want to give your future employer the right impression. You should thank them for their time and consideration after the interview, and you should follow it up by sending an email or a letter once you return home. If you don't do this, the interviewer might believe that you aren't really interested in the job after all.

I hope you have found this guide to interview preparation useful and that carrying through the advice provided in its pages helps your next interview be successful in landing your dream job. Good luck.

References

www.thebalancecareers.com

www.totaljobs.com/insidejob/weird-interview-questions/

http://socialpsychonline.com/2017/05/smile-psychology-science/

https://www.job-hunt.org/job_interviews/avoid-asking-bad-questions.shtml

https://theundercoverrecruiter.com/the-weirdest-interview-questions-how-answer-them-infographic/

Printed in Great Britain
by Amazon